48 LOL

Timeless Secrets to Finding
Peace in a Chaotic World

the 48
Laws of
PEACE

VICTOR O. CARL

Printed in the United States of America.

For more information, or to book an event, contact :
(Email & Website)
http://www.48lol.com
mail to : info@48lol.com

Book design by Joseph Campbell
Cover design by C.J (*D reinforced*)

ISBN – Ebook : 978-1-965849-04-0
ISBN - Paperback : 978-1-965849-03-3
ISBN - Hardcover : 978-1-965849-05-7

First Edition: September 2024

CONTENTS

Thank you so much for purchasing my book!

I'm beyond excited to have you as part of my reading community. Your support truly means the world to me.

If you could kindly take a moment to scan the QR code below and share your honest review on Amazon, it would mean so much.

For those reading the ebook version, please click the link:

Amazon Review Link

Your feedback is invaluable—it helps me improve as a writer and strengthens our community. I genuinely love hearing from you and deeply appreciate your thoughts!

INTRODUCTION

The Pursuit of Peace in a Chaotic World

I n a world that often seems fraught with division, conflict, and relentless noise, peace is a rarity. It's something we long for, yet many find elusive. We think of peace as a distant shore, something to be pursued through external achievements, the resolution of conflicts, or the attainment of a harmonious environment. But what if we have been looking in the wrong places all along?

This book, ***The 48 Laws of Peace***, invites you to reconsider where peace truly originates. It isn't found in the quiet after an argument or the calm of an untroubled life. True peace begins and ends within. It is a state of mind, a choice, a disciplined practice that must be cultivated daily. This book is not about avoiding conflict or silencing the chaos around you, but about learning to be calm amidst the storm, unshakable in your pursuit of tranquility.

The wisdom contained in these pages is timeless. Drawing on ancient Stoic philosophy, particularly the teachings of Epictetus, this book aims to distill complex ideas into practical laws you can apply to your everyday life. The Stoics knew that external events are beyond our control and that the key to peace is mastering our internal responses. Through this lens, The 48 Laws of Peace* offers a roadmap to inner serenity.

In the chapters that follow, each law is paired with a story a historical narrative that brings the law to life. These stories are rooted in reality, illustrating how people throughout history have struggled with, and ultimately triumphed in, their pursuit of peace. From emperors to monks, from leaders to ordinary people, the journey toward peace is one that transcends time, culture, and circumstance.

The Modern Search for Peace

Modern life pulls us in a thousand directions. Technology has made communication instant, but it has also fragmented our attention. Social media encourages constant comparison, fueling envy and dissatisfaction. The pace of life is faster than ever, and with it comes an overwhelming sense of urgency. We are told we must succeed, prove our worth, and rise above our peers only then, we believe, will we find peace.

Yet this approach leaves many feeling empty. The pursuit of external validation, whether through career success, material wealth, or social recognition, often leads not to peace, but to exhaustion. We live with constant pressure, fearful of failing, and anxious about the future. This inner turmoil reflects the turbulence of our outer world, creating a vicious cycle of unrest.

The premise of The 48 Laws of Peace is simple but profound: Peace is not something to be achieved in the future; it is something to be practiced now. It starts with mastering your inner world, accepting what you cannot change, and finding strength in simplicity. Peace is the byproduct of aligning your thoughts, actions, and values with timeless principles.

Why These Laws?

In compiling these 48 laws, I wanted to capture the essence of what it means to live peacefully in a chaotic world. These laws are not abstract or theoretical; they are drawn from real human experiences. They are the result of observing the patterns that emerge when people live in accordance with their inner values, rather than chasing fleeting external rewards.

Take, for instance, *Law 1: Master the Realm Within*. This is the foundation upon which all other laws are built. If you cannot govern your own thoughts and emotions, how can you expect to find peace? This law is about self-discipline and self-awareness. It challenges you to take control of your inner life, to bring order to your mind so that external chaos cannot disturb your equilibrium.

Similarly, *Law 5: Cultivate Indifference to Insults*, reflects a profound Stoic idea, that others' opinions of you are outside your control and should not disturb your peace. Many of us waste emotional energy reacting to criticism or praise, allowing our self-worth to be dictated by external voices. By cultivating indifference to insults, we reclaim our inner calm and fortify our sense of self.

These laws are interconnected, each reinforcing the others. *Law 7: Prioritize the Present Moment*, emphasizes the importance of living fully in the here and now. When we are consumed by regrets about the past or anxieties about the future, peace eludes us. This law encourages mindfulness; a focus on the present as the only moment we can truly control.

Laws such as Seek Harmony in Relationships (Law 9) and Practice Forgiveness (Law 13) reflects the fact that peace is not just an individual pursuit. We are social beings, and the quality of our relationships profoundly impacts our sense of well-being. These laws provide guidance on cultivating healthy, nurturing relationships while avoiding those that drain our spirit.

The Role of Stoicism

Central to this book is the philosophy of Stoicism, an ancient school of thought that teaches the importance of focusing on what we can control and accepting what we cannot. Epictetus, one of the most famous Stoic philosophers, taught that we cannot always control the events that happen to us, but we can control how we respond to them. His teachings form the backbone of "The 48 Laws of Peace".

For the Stoics, peace was not the absence of difficulty or challenge. Rather, it was a state of mind—a calm acceptance of life's impermanence and uncertainty. Stoicism teaches us to let go of attachment to external things—whether success, possessions, or the opinions of others—and instead focus on cultivating inner virtues such as wisdom, courage, and compassion.

This book borrows heavily from Stoic principles, but it is not a purely philosophical text. Instead, it uses these ideas as a framework to explore how ordinary people can apply them to everyday life. The laws in this book are designed to be practical, offering real-world strategies for maintaining peace, even in the midst of life's inevitable difficulties.

A New Approach to Power

While "The 48 Laws of Power" by Robert Greene focuses on how to gain and maintain power in relationships, this book takes a different approach. Power in the traditional sense is about control; over others, over circumstances, over outcomes. But peace requires a relinquishment of that need for control. It asks you to let go, to trust the process of life, and to focus on what is within your sphere of influence.

The goal of "The 48 Laws of Peace" is not to teach you how to dominate or win, but how to find contentment and balance in a world that often feels out of control. This is not to say that peace is passive or weak; far from it. True peace requires inner strength, resilience, and a deep understanding of the self. It is about mastering the most difficult realm of all: the mind.

How to Use This Book

As you read through the laws, I encourage you to reflect on how each one applies to your own life. Peace is not something that can be achieved overnight; it is a lifelong practice. The laws in this book are meant to be guiding principles; tools you can use to navigate the challenges and complexities of modern life.

Each chapter begins with a law, followed by a quote that encapsulates its essence. You will then encounter a story, historical, relatable, and grounded in reality that illustrates how this law has been applied in the past. The aim is to make these ideas come alive, showing how people across time and place have sought peace, often in the most trying circumstances.

Finally, each chapter closes with reflections on how you can integrate the law into your own life. Peace is a practice, not a destination. By incorporating these laws into your daily routine, you can gradually cultivate a state of mind that is calm, centered, and resilient—no matter what life throws your way.

The Promise of Peace

Peace is not a utopia or a far-off dream. It is within reach, for those willing to pursue it. The 48 laws in this book offer a path—a way of being that is aligned with the deeper truths of life. In following them, you will not only find peace within yourself, but you will also become a beacon of peace for others. The world around you may remain turbulent, but you will have mastered the realm within.

This is the promise of *The 48 Laws of Peace.* Let it guide you toward a life of greater harmony, clarity, and contentment. The journey begins within.

Law 1

MASTER THE REALM WITHIN

"He who conquers himself is the mightiest warrior"
- Confucius

In the heart of ancient Rome, where grand marble temples and bustling forums painted the skyline, Marcus Aurelius stood as both a beacon of power and a paragon of philosophical wisdom. As the Roman Emperor, his life was a blend of political might and profound introspection, a juxtaposition that defined his unique approach to leadership.

Marcus Aurelius was not merely a ruler who wielded authority with an iron fist; he was a man deeply committed to the principles of Stoicism. This ancient philosophy, which teaches the development of self-control and fortitude as a means to overcome destructive emotions, was not just an intellectual pursuit for Aurelius but a practical guide for living. His reflections, recorded in his work "Meditations", reveal a ruler who grappled daily with his internal struggles, seeking to align his actions with his values of reason and virtue.

In 165 AD, the Roman Empire faced a grave crisis: the Antonine Plague. This devastating outbreak, likely a form of smallpox or measles, swept through the empire with alarming speed, causing widespread suffering and death. The streets of Rome, usually teeming with activity, grew eerily silent as fear and grief took hold of the population.

During this tumultuous period, Marcus Aurelius's stoic philosophy was put to the ultimate test. As the plague ravaged the city, he could have easily succumbed to panic and despair. The weight of leadership was immense; not only was he responsible for the welfare of millions, but he also had to maintain stability in an empire facing both internal strife and external threats.

Yet, Aurelius exemplified the essence of Stoicism by confronting the crisis with a steadfast inner calm. While the disease claimed lives and strained resources, he remained a figure of unshakable composure. His ability to govern amidst such chaos was a testament to his inner strength. By focusing on what he could control—his responses and actions—he navigated the empire through one of its darkest hours.

In his "Meditations," Aurelius reflected on the nature of suffering and the importance of maintaining personal tranquility. He wrote about the necessity of accepting what we cannot change and diligently working on our own character and actions. These writings were not just philosophical musings but practical guidance that influenced his approach to leadership during the plague.

Aurelius's resolve and measured response to the epidemic helped sustain the morale of his people and provided a model of resilience. His leadership extended beyond mere administrative measures; it was a profound demonstration of how mastering one's inner world can profoundly impact one's ability to manage external crises. Through his calm and reasoned approach, he embodied the core teachings of Stoicism: that true peace and strength come from within, and that by controlling our thoughts and emotions, we can better handle the tumultuous challenges that life presents.

As the plague eventually subsided, Marcus Aurelius's reputation as both a philosopher and a leader was solidified. His legacy endured not just through his conquests or policies, but through the strength of character he displayed during one of the empire's most harrowing periods. In the annals of history, Marcus Aurelius remains a symbol of how inner mastery and philosophical wisdom can guide even the most powerful rulers through the stormiest seas.

True peace begins within. Govern your thoughts, control your desires, and cultivate a spirit of contentment. External conflict often mirrors internal disarray, bringing order to your inner world to bring peace to your outer one. And that is the truth, one of the most difficult things for any person to do is to learn how to master themself; keep their emotions in check, and learn contentment.

Peace might be a difficult thing to find if you are a person who finds solace in external things rather than in yourself. If we want to have a peaceful life, we must ensure that we learn how to be content, many people think to be content is not to want more. This is not true, you can be content and want more out of life, you just have to learn how to be grateful for what you have and work hard to get to where you want to be.

The truth is, when there is so much internal conflict going on within you, you will be restless, irritable and have no peace. This is why you need to learn how to bring peace to your inner world to bring peace to your outer world. Reflection and meditation is a great way to settle inner conflict. Look for a silent place where you can think, and keep a journal beside you. Reflect on your life, what you have been doing, and what you think you should do differently. Write in your journal the things you are reflecting on, meditate on what you have reflected on and you will start to notice a quiet to the noise in your inner being and gradually you will begin to experience peace.

True peace is not about changing external situations and circumstances but about mastering the realm within. Finding joy in the littlest things and letting go of negative emotions can help us settle our inner chaos and experience peace on a greater level. The state of your inner being determines the overall state of your person.

It is very important to pay attention to what is happening inside you, and always look inward whenever you sense that you cannot find your peace. You will notice that immediately after you sort out whatever is causing you inner chaos, you will find peace. Like Confucius said, "Conquer yourself". It might seem difficult but it is attainable.

Law 2

EMBRACE WHAT YOU CANNOT CHANGE

"What we can control is our attitude towards what we cannot control"- Epictetus

In the turbulent landscape of apartheid-era South Africa, Nelson Mandela emerged as a figure of immense courage and unwavering resolve. Imprisoned for 27 long years, Mandela's journey from a political prisoner to a symbol of peace and reconciliation is a testament to the power of inner strength and the profound impact of embracing what one cannot change.

Mandela's imprisonment began in 1962 when he was arrested

for his involvement in the anti-apartheid movement. His incarceration was a brutal experience, marked by harsh conditions and a relentless struggle against a system that sought to suppress his ideals and those of his comrades. For nearly three decades, Mandela endured the dehumanizing effects of imprisonment, far from his family and his home.

Yet, amidst the oppressive confines of Robben Island and other prisons, Mandela chose a path of acceptance and inner fortitude. He understood that while he could not alter the fact of his imprisonment or the injustices of apartheid, he could control his responses and maintain his dignity. This mindset was crucial in sustaining him through the long years of confinement.

Mandela's ability to foster positive relationships with fellow inmates and prison guards was a testament to his strength of character. He refused to allow bitterness or resentment to consume him. Instead, he focused on the elements within his control: nurturing camaraderie with other prisoners, engaging in self-education, and fostering a sense of hope for the future. His demeanor and actions demonstrated an acceptance of his situation, coupled with an unwavering commitment to his larger goal of justice and equality.

During these years, Mandela found solace in his own mental and emotional resilience. His acceptance was not passive resignation but an active engagement with the present moment, allowing him to maintain a sense of peace despite external chaos. This inner tranquility became a crucial source of strength, enabling him to endure the hardships and emerge as a beacon of hope.

Upon his release in 1990, Nelson Mandela faced a South Africa deeply scarred by years of racial segregation and conflict. Many expected him to seek revenge against those who had oppressed him and his people. However, Mandela's approach was fundamentally different. His focus was on reconciliation and healing, reflecting the same spirit of acceptance and transformation he had embraced during his imprisonment.

Mandela's leadership was marked by a profound commitment to national unity and peace. He worked tirelessly to dismantle the legacy of apartheid and to guide South Africa through a transition towards democracy. His decision to forgive his oppressors and his efforts to build bridges between divided communities were not only acts of political strategy but also reflections of his philosophy of acceptance and peace.

In his presidency and beyond, Mandela's influence was a powerful force for reconciliation. He understood that the path to a unified nation required not just political change but a profound shift in the collective mindset. His ability to embrace what he could not change—his past suffering and the complexities of transitioning from a divided society—became a model for others. Mandela's life and leadership illustrated how mastering one's internal world could lead to transformative external outcomes.

Nelson Mandela's legacy is a compelling narrative of resilience and grace. His journey from imprisonment to becoming South Africa's first Black president is a testament to the power of embracing inner peace and using it as a force for broader social change. His story continues to inspire those who face their challenges, demonstrating that true strength lies in accepting and mastering what is within oneself.

Do not waste energy on what lies beyond your control. Accept fate with grace, and focus on what you can influence. Peace arises from the alignment of your will with the natural course of events. Embracing what you cannot change is usually easier said than done. This does not make the saying untrue, although it can be quite difficult.

You will not be able to control every situation, however, there is one thing that you can always control and that is your attitude towards the situation. You can by the reason of practice and training control your attitude such that you can always predict how you will react to any situation. Embracing what you cannot change takes discipline and intentionality, you must make up your mind that you will never allow what you cannot change to steal your peace.

There is a level of peace you will enjoy when you come to understand that you cannot change everything. This does not mean that you are nonchalant or you are not concerned about the situation. It just means that you have found a way to stop things and situations that are beyond your control from stealing your peace and joy.

It also means that you are in control of the situation, and your emotions are not flying everywhere. This gives you leverage; you will be able to think about how well you should handle the situation. Level-headed people have been known to make the right decisions even in the toughest situations. The ability to focus on what you can influence is one that everyone can build. You have to make a choice. "I choose to focus on what I can influence", and "I choose to accept fate with grace", are decisions you must be willing to make. When you start to focus your energy on better things, you will start to experience positive results and enjoy your life better. It is unfruitful to focus your energy on things and situations you cannot change. Spend your time building new opportunities for yourself, building resilience, grace, and grit. Peace comes from aligning our will to the natural course of events.

Law 3

FIND STRENGTH IN SIMPLICITY

"Simplicity is the ultimate sophistication"-Leonardo Da Vinci

In the summer of 1845, Henry David Thoreau embarked on a personal experiment that would come to define his philosophical and literary legacy. Seeking to live a life of simplicity and purpose, Thoreau retreated to a small cabin he built near Walden Pond in Concord, Massachusetts. His goal was clear: to strip away the extraneous and embrace a life deeply connected to nature, self-reliance, and introspection.

Thoreau's decision to live at Walden Pond was more than a mere escape from society; it was a deliberate choice to engage with the fundamentals of existence. The cabin he constructed was modest, a humble abode with minimal furnishings, reflecting his desire to simplify his surroundings. Thoreau's home was not just a physical shelter but a symbolic retreat from the complexities of modern life.

Living off the land, Thoreau cultivated a small garden, foraged for wild food, and embraced the rhythm of nature. His days were filled with the routines of manual labor, observation of the natural world, and deep contemplation. He wrote extensively about his experiences and reflections in his journal, which would later form the basis of his seminal work, *Walden*.

Thoreau's time at Walden Pond was marked by a profound immersion in the natural environment. He meticulously observed the changing seasons, the behavior of animals, and the interplay of light and water. These observations were not mere scientific inquiries but meditations on the interconnectedness of life and the essence of simplicity. Through this close engagement with nature, Thoreau discovered a clarity and peace that transcended the distractions and pressures of contemporary society.

In "Walden", Thoreau articulates the philosophical underpinnings of his experiment. He argues that modern life, with its constant pursuit of material wealth and social status, often obscures the true essence of living. By focusing on the essentials—nature, thought, and self-reliance—Thoreau found a deeper sense of fulfillment and understanding. His writings reveal that simplicity is not about deprivation but about recognizing and embracing what truly matters.

The lessons Thoreau learned at Walden Pond extended beyond his own life. His reflections on the virtues of simplicity, self-sufficiency, and a closer connection to nature have inspired countless readers and thinkers. "Walden" is not just a record of

Thoreau's personal journey but a timeless exploration of how to live deliberately and authentically.

Thoreau's experiment at Walden Pond remains a powerful testament to the strength found in simplicity. His ability to find peace and clarity by removing the superfluous aspects of life offers a compelling argument for the value of living intentionally. His experiences encourage us to reflect on our own lives, to consider what we can remove to make space for what truly enriches our existence.

In the decades since Thoreau's time at Walden Pond, his writings have continued to resonate with those who seek to simplify their lives and reconnect with the essentials. His legacy endures as a reminder that amidst the complexity of modern life, there is profound wisdom to be found in the quiet, deliberate embrace of simplicity and nature.

Complication breeds confusion and disquiet. Simplify your life—your actions, your desires, your possessions. The simpler your existence, the more profound your peace. As humans, we feel the need to be sophisticated whereas simplicity is key. It relieves you of unnecessary stress and allows you to enjoy a great quality of life. If you are someone who likes to be involved in everything and anything, attend different programs, meetings and social events, go to work, honour your commitments and do several other things, there is a probability that you will always be tired and stressed.

Also, working or living in a cluttered space is not helpful for your mental health; cluttered spaces are usually a distraction, making you feel overwhelmed, anxious and stressed. In conclusion, a cluttered space hinders your productivity. A decluttered space helps you to think better, focus on essential tasks and priorities. Simplicity has a way of reducing mental clutters, minimizing distractions, fostering clarity, calmness, sense of control and direction.

If your workload is too much, it can impact your inner being and cause you to feel overwhelmed and burnt out. Reducing your workload can help to decrease stress and anxiety, allow for free time and relaxation, help give you a work-life balance and enhance your overall happiness. When you simplify your life; your actions, your desires and your possession by reducing your workload, decluttering your space, focus on meaningful relationships and attend meetings and social events that are important, you will start to experience an increase in tranquility, enhanced creativity and productivity.

Embracing simplicity, helps you to nurture an environment where peace can thrive. Complications have no advantage; it will only breed confusion and chaos. Resist from living a complex life; simplicity is sophistication, it speaks of class and elegance. When you live a simple and uncomplicated life, it shows that you are focused and have a sense of direction.

Law 4

PRACTICE DELIBERATE RESTRAINT

"He who is brave is free." - *Seneca*

In the tumultuous days of ancient Rome, amidst the shifting tides of political power and military strife, the figure of Lucius Quinctius Cincinnatus stands out as a paragon of self-restraint and civic virtue. His story, set in 458 BC, is a compelling testament to the ideals of leadership and the rare quality of relinquishing power for the greater good.

At this critical juncture, Rome faced a dire threat. Enemy forces were advancing on the city, and the Republic was in desperate need of strong leadership. In response to the crisis, the Roman Senate appointed Cincinnatus as dictator, a role that granted him extraordinary powers to lead Rome's defense. Cincinnatus, who had retired from public life and was tending his modest farm, was a man of integrity known for his dedication to the Republic.

Upon his appointment, Cincinnatus demonstrated remarkable decisiveness and strategic acumen. He left his farm, where he lived a life of simplicity and hard work, and took command of

Rome's military forces. His leadership was characterized by a blend of tactical brilliance and calm resolve. He swiftly organized and led Rome's armies to victory against the invading forces, securing the city's safety and stabilizing the Republic during a time of peril.

What set Cincinnatus apart from other leaders of his time was his profound sense of duty and restraint. Despite the vast powers vested in him as dictator, Cincinnatus did not seek to extend his authority beyond the immediate crisis. The temptation to consolidate power, to transform his temporary role into a more permanent one, was ever-present in a period marked by political ambition and intrigue. Yet, Cincinnatus resisted this allure.

Once the immediate threat was quelled and Rome was secure, Cincinnatus made a momentous decision. True to his principles, he voluntarily relinquished his dictatorial powers and returned to his life as a farmer. This act of self-restraint was extraordinary in the context of Roman politics, where many leaders sought to retain power and manipulate the system for personal gain. Cincinnatus's willingness to step down from a position of immense authority underscored his commitment to the principles of civic duty and the rule of law.

His return to the simplicity of his farm after such a high-stakes role was not an act of retreat but a statement of his values. Cincinnatus's actions exemplified the ideal of the Roman citizen-soldier—one who serves the Republic out of a sense of duty and then returns to private life, leaving behind the trappings of power.

The legacy of Lucius Quinctius Cincinnatus endured long after his time. His story became a powerful symbol of virtuous leadership and self-restraint. In later centuries, Cincinnatus was celebrated by Roman historians and political leaders as an exemplar of how true leadership involves acting decisively when needed and stepping aside when one's role is fulfilled. His life was an enduring lesson that the strength of character lies not just in wielding power but in the wisdom to relinquish it for the sake of the greater good.

In the annals of Roman history, Cincinnatus remains a revered figure whose example continues to inspire those who value integrity and civic responsibility over personal ambition. His story serves as a timeless reminder of the profound impact that self-restraint and dedication to public service can have on the stability and moral fabric of a society.

Resist the urge to react impulsively. Consider your words and actions carefully, for hasty decisions often lead to unnecessary conflict. Restraint is a shield that guards your peace.
When you carefully consider your actions and words, you will be able to defuse tension and approach conflicts with a calm demeanor. Your deliberate restraint will not only preserve your peace but improve your relationships.

Careful consideration often prevents unnecessary strife; think before you act. Restraint is a shield that guards your peace; it helps you conserve your mental and emotional energy for the things that truly matter. Don't act on impulse, always remember to take a deep breath and think well before saying anything. One thing you must not lose is your peace, ensure you do all it takes to ensure that your peace is intact. Create space for growth, learning and self care. One of the things you should do to ensure your peace is intact is to learn how to restrain yourself, preserve your energy and shield yourself from negative and toxic emotions. Restraint is about intentional living, prioritizing your peace and living a calm and fulfilling life.

Law 5

CULTIVATE INDIFFERENCE TO INSULTS

"It is not things themselves that disturb us, but our interpretation of those things." - Epictetus.

Mahatma Gandhi, a pivotal figure in India's struggle for independence, is renowned not only for his leadership but also for his profound dedication to the principle of nonviolence. His journey was marked by numerous challenges, including personal insults and provocations from both British colonial rulers and critics within his own country. Through it all, Gandhi's unwavering commitment to nonviolence and his ability to maintain his inner peace played a crucial role in leading India to independence.

Gandhi's path to becoming a champion of nonviolence was shaped by his experiences and philosophical reflections. When he returned to India from South Africa in the early 1910s, he was already an advocate for civil rights and social reform, having pioneered nonviolent resistance against discriminatory practices in South Africa. This experience laid the groundwork for his approach to India's fight against British colonial rule.

As he emerged as a leader in the Indian independence movement, Gandhi faced relentless opposition and hostility. The British colonial authorities, accustomed to enforcing their rule through force and coercion, viewed Gandhi's nonviolent resistance with disdain and attempted to discredit him through various means. Similarly, some within India, who were skeptical of Gandhi's methods or who had differing political agendas, challenging his principles and questioned his leadership.

Despite these provocations, Gandhi remained steadfast in his commitment to nonviolence, a principle he described as "ahimsa". For Gandhi, nonviolence was not merely a strategic choice but a profound moral conviction. It involved not only abstaining from physical violence but also refraining from harboring hatred or anger. He believed that true power lay in the ability to respond to hostility with compassion and to confront injustice without perpetuating further violence.

Gandhi's response to insults and provocations was marked by remarkable forbearance. He understood that external insults and criticisms did not reflect his true self and chose not to be swayed by them. Instead of retaliating or seeking revenge, Gandhi focused on his mission and remained resolute in his principles. This indifference to personal attacks allowed him to preserve his inner peace and moral authority.

One notable instance of Gandhi's resilience was during the salt march of 1930, a pivotal event in the struggle against British rule. As Gandhi and his followers marched to the Arabian Sea to produce salt in defiance of British regulations, they faced not only physical hardships but also verbal abuse and hostility from various quarters. Yet, Gandhi's response to these provocations remained consistent with his philosophy. He used these challenges as opportunities to demonstrate the power of nonviolence and the strength of the movement he led.

Gandhi's ability to maintain his composure and adhere to his principles in the face of adversity contributed significantly to the moral high ground of the Indian independence movement. His approach inspired millions to join the cause and adopt nonviolent methods in their own struggles. Gandhi's steadfastness in the face of personal attacks helped unify the movement and build a collective resolve for change.

Ultimately, Gandhi's indifference to insults and his adherence to nonviolence were instrumental in achieving India's independence in 1947. His legacy endures as a powerful example of how inner peace and moral conviction can overcome the most formidable challenges. Gandhi's life and work demonstrate that true strength lies in the ability to rise above personal grievances and focus on a higher purpose, using nonviolence as a force for profound social and political transformation.

Mahatma Gandhi's story is a testament to the power of maintaining one's principles amidst adversity. His unwavering commitment to nonviolence and his capacity to remain undisturbed by insults and provocations continue to inspire those who seek to make a difference in the world through peaceful means.

The opinions of others are their own; they do not define you. Let insults roll off like water from a stone. By not engaging with provocation, you maintain your tranquility. You can choose how you see things, how you interpret things and how those things affect you. Many times we find ourselves in a web of hurt, anger and hatred triggered by someone's thoughtless words. We begin to find ways to avoid these insults and the person hurling it. You must come to understand that insults are a reflection of the person hurling them not you. Through their insults, you can get a glimpse into their insecurities, biases and limitations.

Other people's words are not the definition of your worth and identity. You give definition and identity to yourself. Don't be a sponge soaking up other people's negativity, be indifferent, unshakable and strong. Break free from the weight of other people's opinion and define who you are.

Whenever we engage in provocation, we are directly surrendering our peace. When we respond to insults by retaliating or reacting, we give power to those provoking us. It does not end there, we also waste our energy on unnecessary conflict and we risk losing ourselves. Indifference is the conscious effort to rise above noise. By ignoring insults, you protect your mental and emotional well being, radiate confidence, maintain focus and ensure you do not lose your peace.

You can learn indifference by understanding the insecurities and limitations of others, engaging in insults only when it is necessary and doing it with calmness. Another way to learn indifference is to see insults as an opportunity to grow and learn. Remember that insults and criticisms are a reflection of your provocateur's perspective and not a judgment of your true value.

Indifference sets you free from the opinion of others. Refuse to be shaken by insults, detach your self worth from external validation, radiate confidence, focus on your journey and walk taller. By doing this, you will protect your inner peace and continue to live life with continued peace and joy

Law 6

FOCUS ON YOUR SPHERE OF CONTROL

"The more we value things outside our control, the less control we have."- Epictetus.

Epictetus, born into slavery around 50 AD in the Roman Empire, is a profound example of how personal philosophy can transform one's life and impact the world. Despite the harsh realities of his early life, Epictetus rose to become one of the most influential Stoic philosophers, renowned for his teachings on focusing only on what is within our control.

Epictetus was initially a slave to a wealthy Roman named Epaphroditus. His early life was marked by the constraints and indignities of slavery, a condition that could easily have fostered bitterness and despair. Yet, Epictetus's response to his circumstances reflected the core principles of Stoicism—a philosophy that teaches the development of self-control and rationality as a means to overcome life's adversities.

From a young age, Epictetus demonstrated a remarkable ability to maintain his inner peace despite external conditions. His resilience and philosophical outlook were evident in his teachings, which emphasized that true freedom and happiness come not from changing external circumstances but from mastering one's internal state. Epictetus famously taught that individuals should focus on what they can control—namely their own actions, thoughts, and responses—while accepting with equanimity what they cannot change.

When Epictetus was eventually freed from slavery, his commitment to Stoic philosophy deepened. He began to teach and lecture on Stoic principles, attracting a significant following. His teachings, primarily preserved through the works of his student Arrian, centered on the idea that while we may not have control over external events or the actions of others, we have complete control over our own responses and attitudes.

One of the central tenets of Epictetus's philosophy is the distinction between what is within our power and what is not. He argued that we should focus our efforts solely on what we can influence—our own behavior, judgments, and reactions—while accepting the inevitability of things beyond our control. This focus on personal responsibility and inner strength was not just theoretical for Epictetus; it was a principle he lived by, accepting his circumstances without complaint and using his experiences to cultivate his character and wisdom.

Epictetus's teachings were not merely academic; they offered practical guidance for everyday living. His emphasis on personal discipline, rational thinking, and emotional resilience resonated with many and provided a framework for achieving inner peace amidst life's challenges. His ideas on accepting fate and focusing on internal virtues have had a lasting impact, inspiring countless individuals to adopt a Stoic approach to life.

The enduring influence of Epictetus's philosophy is a testament to his ability to turn personal adversity into a source of profound insight and guidance. His teachings continue to be studied and revered for their practical wisdom and emphasis on the power of individual agency. By concentrating on what we can control and letting go of concerns beyond our influence, Epictetus provided a pathway to peace and self-mastery that remains relevant to this day.

Epictetus's life and philosophy illustrate how even in the face of significant personal and societal limitations, one can achieve greatness and make a lasting impact by adhering to core principles of self-discipline and rationality. His legacy endures as a beacon for those seeking to navigate life's complexities with grace and resilience.

Peace is found in knowing where your influence ends. Do not fret over the uncontrollable; instead, channel your energy into what you can shape. Your peace grows as you withdraw from futile struggles. True peace lies in focusing on what you can control. The world is filled with uncertainty and chaos, you can get caught up in trying to control everything about you and this can be futile and exhausting.

Most of us spend our time and energy worrying over things we cannot control. In truth, our stress and anxiety stems from trying to control what is beyond us. It is very important that we distinguish between what we can control and what we cannot. We can control our thoughts and attitude, our actions and reactions, and our values and goals. Every other thing is beyond our sphere of control. When we focus on what we can control we conserve our energy, reduce stress and anxiety, increase our productivity and effectiveness and cultivate our inner peace and calm.

While it is not easy to let go, it can be very liberating. We need to release ourselves from the need to control everything, we are only men. When we learn to control only what is within our influence, we will break free from worry and fear, open ourselves to new opportunities and possibilities and develop a sense of acceptance and trust.

The first step to focusing on your sphere of control is to
- Identify what you can and cannot control.

- Focus and pay attention to only what you can control.

- Release the need to always be in control of everything, let it go!

- Recognize when you start to step into futile struggles.

- Pour your energy into what you can change.

Learn to concentrate on your own actions, let others account for theirs, trust others to handle their own responsibilities, and shift your perspective to know that you cannot change or control everything. When you learn to focus on your sphere of influence, you will find peace. Your energy is precious and your peace is worth protecting. Like Epictetus said, it is not what happens to you, it is how you react to it.

Law 7

PRIORITIZE THE PRESENT MOMENT

"The present is the only time we have control over."
- Epictetus.

Hakuin Ekaku, a revered Japanese Zen master of the 18th century, is celebrated for his profound insights into the practice of mindfulness and the importance of living fully in the present moment. His teachings, which emphasize the necessity of anchoring oneself in the here and now, have left an indelible mark on Zen Buddhism and continue to inspire countless individuals on their spiritual journeys.

Born in 1686 in Hara, Japan, Hakuin's early life was marked by a restless search for spiritual meaning. Initially drawn to various Buddhist traditions, he eventually encountered Zen, which profoundly shaped his path. His journey to enlightenment was characterized by a rigorous commitment to meditation and mindfulness, through which he developed a deep understanding of Zen principles.

Central to Hakuin's teachings was the idea that true peace and enlightenment are found not by escaping the present moment but by immersing oneself fully in it. He taught that many of the struggles and distractions that prevent individuals from achieving inner peace stem from an inability to focus on the here and now. Dwelling on past regrets or worrying about future uncertainties only serves to distance one from the present, which is where true clarity and tranquility reside.

Hakuin's approach to meditation was both intense and transformative. He advocated for a practice known as "koan" meditation, which involves contemplating paradoxical questions or statements to transcend ordinary thinking and attain a direct experience of reality. This method, while seemingly paradoxical, was designed to cut through conceptual barriers and bring practitioners to a profound awareness of the present moment.

One of the key aspects of Hakuin's teachings was his emphasis on the immediacy of enlightenment. He often used vivid and sometimes dramatic language to convey that the potential for awakening is available in every moment, and it is through direct engagement with the present that one can experience this profound realization. Hakuin himself exemplified this through his own disciplined practice and the clarity he demonstrated in his teachings.

His teachings were not limited to the confines of monastic practice but extended to everyday life. Hakuin encouraged his students to integrate mindfulness into all aspects of their lives, emphasizing that spiritual awakening is not confined to formal meditation sessions but should permeate every action and thought. By focusing on the present moment and letting go of distractions, individuals could find a deeper connection to themselves and their surroundings.

One notable aspect of Hakuin's legacy is his influence on the revival of Zen Buddhism in Japan. His teachings inspired a renewed interest in Zen practice, and his methods became foundational for many Zen practitioners. His writings, including his "Orategama" (the "Jewel Mirror of the True Mind") and various recorded sayings, continue to be studied and revered for their profound insights into the nature of mind and presence.

Through his life and work, Hakuin Ekaku demonstrated how the practice of mindfulness and the focus on the present moment can lead to profound peace and enlightenment. His teachings offer a timeless reminder of the importance of living fully in the here and now, and his legacy endures as a guiding light for those seeking to cultivate a deeper sense of presence and awareness in their own lives.

In essence, Hakuin's approach to Zen was not merely about meditative techniques but about transforming one's relationship with time and awareness. His insistence on the value of the present moment provides a powerful tool for overcoming the distractions of daily life and discovering the profound serenity that lies within each moment.

Peace is the fruit of living fully in the present. The past is gone, the future uncertain—anchor yourself in the now. By focusing on the present, you diminish anxiety and increase contentment. This saying is true. Life will teach you again and again that the present is the only time you have control over. What is gone is gone, what has happened has happened, you can only work hard to control today.

Many of us, spent years regretting what has happened, refusing to move on from the past. The past is what it is "The past"! You will only waste your time if you try to change what happened yesterday or years ago. You can't even change what happened a few minutes ago. Why waste your time crying over spilled milk when you can focus on now.

When you focus on now, you reduce your anxiety and stress levels. Worrying over what you cannot control will only make you anxious and increase your blood pressure. Your contentment and gratitude will increase when you come to understand that all you can control is the present. Your sense of calm and clarity will be enhanced and your focus and concentration will improve because you have decided to focus your energy and strength on what you can control.

You can anchor yourself in the now by taking a few minutes everyday to focus on your breath and the present moment. Let go of the past and hold on to the future. Appreciating the goodness and the beauty in your life presently can help you to focus on the present. Focus on today and leave tomorrow to worry about itself.

A sense of peace that is not dependent on external things will become your experience when you learn to trust in the unfolding of life, build inner strength and resilience, and find joy in your journey not your destination. You will find peace by living in the present.

Law 8

CHOOSE YOUR BATTLES WISELY

"A wise man fights not to win, but to gain peace."- *Epictetus*

In 1259 BC, the ancient world witnessed a landmark event in diplomatic history: the signing of the Treaty of Kadesh. This treaty, between the Egyptian Pharaoh Ramses II and the Hittite King Hattusili III, stands as one of the earliest recorded peace agreements and exemplifies the wisdom of choosing peace over protracted conflict.

The Treaty of Kadesh emerged from a period of intense and prolonged warfare between Egypt and the Hittite Empire, two of the most formidable powers of the time. The conflicts between these two empires, primarily over the control of territory in the region of modern-day Syria, had caused significant devastation and strained both nations' resources.

The central battle of this prolonged conflict was the Battle of Kadesh, fought around 1274 BC. Despite both sides claiming victory, the battle did not lead to a decisive end to the hostilities.

Instead, it left both empires exhausted and in a precarious position. The realization began to dawn that continuing the war would only lead to further mutual destruction, without any clear benefit for either side.

Recognizing the futility of continued warfare, Ramses II and Hattusili III opted for negotiation rather than further bloodshed. The Treaty of Kadesh was signed in 1259 BC, and it marked a significant turning point in ancient diplomacy. This treaty was remarkable not only for its early date but also for its contents and the principles it established.

The treaty's terms included mutual recognition of each other's sovereignty, a commitment to non-aggression, and the establishment of diplomatic relations. Importantly, it included provisions for the return of prisoners and a clause to assist each other in the event of future threats. This mutual respect and cooperation were designed to ensure that the peace would be lasting and beneficial for both parties.

The Treaty of Kadesh was inscribed on stelae and carved into temple walls, ensuring that the agreement was publicly recorded and honored by both empires. This form of documentation helped to cement the treaty's importance and serve as a historical record of the diplomatic triumph.

The treaty's significance extends beyond its immediate historical context. It serves as a powerful example of the strategic wisdom in choosing when to seek peace rather than pursuing victory at all costs. By opting for negotiation and compromise, Ramses II and Hattusili III preserved their empires and avoided further devastation. The treaty illustrated the potential for diplomacy to resolve conflicts and maintain stability, even among powerful and rival states.

Furthermore, the Treaty of Kadesh set a precedent for future diplomatic agreements. It demonstrated that even in a world dominated by martial prowess and territorial ambitions, there was a place for formal treaties and negotiations to address disputes and foster long-term peace. The principles established in this early treaty continued to influence diplomatic practices in subsequent centuries.

The Treaty of Kadesh remains a testament to the enduring value of diplomacy and the strategic decision to seek peace. Its legacy highlights the importance of resolving conflicts through dialogue and mutual respect, offering a timeless lesson in the art of statecraft and the pursuit of lasting harmony.

In essence, the Treaty of Kadesh exemplifies how recognizing the limits of warfare and choosing to negotiate can lead to a more stable and prosperous future for all parties involved. The agreement stands as a historical milestone that underscores the importance of peace and diplomacy in maintaining the stability of civilizations.

Not every conflict is worth engaging. Preserve your peace by discerning which battles truly matter. The wise walk away from unnecessary strife, keeping their energy for what is essential. It is not wise to fight every battle because you will lose your peace. The truth is not every battle is worth fighting, it is wise to walk away from unnecessary argument and conflict. Your energy should be spent on what truly matters and not irrelevancies.

When you engage in constant drama and conflict, you will notice that you feel drained and depleted. It is important to know when to stand your ground and when to walk away. Engaging in unnecessary conflict will cause you emotional exhaustion, strained relationships, decreased productivity and your peace and happiness will be eroded.

Discernment plays an important role in preserving your peace and energy; not every battle is worth it. There are three questions you should ask yourself before engaging in a conflict.

- Does this conflict align with my values and goals?

- Is this conflict worth the investment of my time and energy?

- Can this conflict be resolved without compromising my integrity?

Choose your battle wisely by establishing for yourself what you are willing or not willing to engage, this serves as a guide to inform what conflict you should engage in. When you focus on what is truly important to you, you will notice that you will not engage minor issues.

Another way to choose your battle is to learn to walk away. When there is an unnecessary strife, walk away. Not every issue is worth your time. When you choose your battles wisely you preserve your peace and energy, build stronger and more meaningful relationships, increase your productivity and focus, and build your resilience.

Law 9

SEEK HARMONY IN RELATIONSHIPS

"We are more concerned about our own peace than we are about the peace of those around us." - *Epictetus.*

The Iroquois Confederacy, also known as the Haudenosaunee or Six Nations, stands as a remarkable example of how seeking harmony in relationships can forge a powerful and enduring political alliance. Formed between the 12th and 15th centuries, this confederacy united five, and later six, Native American tribes in the northeastern part of what is now the United States. The principles and structures of the Confederacy, enshrined in the Great Law of Peace, exemplify the value of consensus-building, mutual respect, and unity in maintaining a stable and influential political entity.

The origins of the Iroquois Confederacy are rooted in a period of considerable inter-tribal conflict. Before the Confederacy was established, the region was marked by frequent wars and disputes among the Iroquois tribes, including the Mohawk,

Oneida, Onondaga, Cayuga, and Seneca. This era of turmoil highlighted the need for a new approach to governance and conflict resolution.

The formation of the Confederacy is traditionally attributed to a visionary leader known as Dekanawida, or the Great Peacemaker, and his ally Hiawatha. Their efforts were instrumental in proposing and implementing a new system of governance based on principles of peace and cooperation. The result was the Great Law of Peace, a comprehensive set of laws and guidelines designed to promote harmony among the member tribes and address disputes through peaceful means.

The Great Law of Peace emphasized several key principles:
1. Consensus-Building: Decisions within the Confederacy were made through a process of consensus rather than by majority rule. Each tribe had a voice in discussions, and decisions required broad agreement. This approach ensured that the interests and perspectives of all member tribes were considered, fostering a sense of collective ownership and commitment to the outcomes.

2. Mutual Respect: The Confederacy was founded on the principle of mutual respect among the tribes. The Great Law of Peace enshrined the idea that each tribe retained its own identity and autonomy while working together for the common good. This respect for diversity and individuality within the Confederacy was crucial in maintaining harmonious

relationships and preventing conflict.

3. Maintaining Harmony: The Confederacy's governance structure was designed to promote and sustain peace. The leaders, known as sachems, were chosen based on their wisdom and ability to mediate conflicts. They played a key role in upholding the principles of the Great Law of Peace and ensuring that disputes were resolved through dialogue rather than warfare.

The effectiveness of the Iroquois Confederacy in achieving stability and power can be seen in its longevity and influence. For centuries, the Confederacy remained a dominant and respected political entity in pre-colonial North America. Its system of governance provided a model of cooperative politics and conflict resolution that was notable for its sophistication and effectiveness.

The Confederacy also played a significant role in interactions with European settlers and colonial powers. Its diplomatic and strategic acumen enabled it to navigate complex relationships with various European nations, balancing alliances and treaties to protect its interests and maintain its sovereignty.

The legacy of the Iroquois Confederacy extends beyond its historical period. The principles enshrined in the Great Law of Peace continue to inspire and inform contemporary discussions on governance, conflict resolution, and community building.

The Confederacy's emphasis on consensus, respect, and harmony serves as a timeless reminder of the power of collaborative leadership and the importance of seeking peaceful solutions.

In summary, the Iroquois Confederacy stands as a testament to the effectiveness of seeking harmony in relationships. Its enduring success as a political entity reflects the strength of its foundational principles and the wisdom of its leaders. The Great Law of Peace not only shaped the Confederacy's internal dynamics but also set a standard for how diverse groups can work together to achieve lasting stability and prosperity.

Peace is not isolation but harmonious interaction. Cultivate relationships that nurture your spirit and avoid those that drain it. Surround yourself with those who contribute to your peace. Relationships are meant to be harmonious, many times we forget that harmony is key in any relationship. Surround yourself with relationships that nurture your spirit and you should also nurture your friend's spirit too. Avoid those who drain you and don't drain others.

To enjoy a level of peace in any relationship, all parties involved must be willing to invest positive energy to the relationship. Anytime you feel drained and stressed after interacting with certain people, cut them off. The company you keep has a profound impact on your well being. You can only find peace in a harmonious relationship. Surround yourself with people who boost your mood, energy and provide emotional support. Your relationships should foster learning and personal growth, enhance your connection and sense of belonging. Any relationship that does the opposite of what was mentioned earlier, should be cut off. Toxic relationships will drain you, steal your joy and peace, cause you stress and anxiety, erode your self-esteem and confidence. You will start to doubt yourself; you won't be able to reach your full potential and it will steal your happiness. There are several ways you can set a harmonious relationship. First is to set clear boundaries; say no to relationships that drain you. If you need to give space to a certain "stella" that refuses to move on, please do. Secondly, ensure that you build relationships with people who share your values and interests. Be an active listener, learn to see things from other people's perspectives. Only invest time and energy in relationships that are uplifting and lastly, be yourself! None and nothing is worth losing yourself for. Surround yourself with people that contribute to your peace.

Law 10

REFLECT BEFORE YOU ACT

"It is not the action itself, but the reflection before it that determines its worth." - Epictetus

In October 1962, the world faced one of its gravest crisis, teetering on the edge of nuclear war during the Cuban Missile Crisis. This intense standoff between the United States and the Soviet Union was triggered by the discovery of Soviet ballistic missiles in Cuba, just 90 miles from the U.S. coast. The crisis is a powerful example of how thoughtful and measured decision-making can prevent catastrophic conflict.

The Cuban Missile Crisis began when U.S. reconnaissance flights over Cuba revealed that the Soviet Union, under the leadership of Nikita Khrushchev, had secretly installed nuclear missiles on the island. These missiles posed a direct threat to the United States, capable of reaching major cities within minutes. The discovery led to immediate concern within the U.S. government, as the missiles could potentially alter the balance of power in the Cold War.

President John F. Kennedy, facing the prospect of a potential nuclear conflict, was thrust into a high-stakes situation that demanded both immediate action and careful deliberation. The pressure on Kennedy was immense, as he needed to balance the need for a decisive response with the need to avoid escalating the situation into full-scale war.

Rather than opting for an immediate military strike, which would have likely provoked a severe Soviet response and risked triggering nuclear retaliation, Kennedy chose a more measured approach. He convened a series of meetings with his closest advisors, known as the Executive Committee of the National Security Council (ExComm), to thoroughly discuss and evaluate the options available.

Kennedy's decision-making process was marked by careful reflection and restraint. He understood that the stakes were extraordinarily high, and any action needed to be carefully considered to avoid unintended escalation. After deliberation, Kennedy and his advisors decided on a naval blockade, or "quarantine," of Cuba. This measure was designed to prevent further Soviet shipments of military equipment to the island without immediately resorting to military action.

In addition to the blockade, Kennedy pursued diplomatic negotiations with the Soviet leadership. The goal was to resolve the crisis through dialogue rather than conflict. Kennedy communicated directly with Khrushchev, seeking a peaceful resolution while making it clear that the U.S. would not tolerate the continued presence of Soviet missiles in Cuba.

Kennedy's measured approach also involved public communication. On October 22, he addressed the American public and the world, revealing the existence of the missiles and the U.S. response. His calm and composed demeanor helped to maintain public confidence and avoid unnecessary panic.

The combination of the naval blockade and diplomatic negotiations proved effective. The Soviet Union, recognizing the risk of a full-scale war and the strength of the U.S. response, eventually agreed to remove the missiles from Cuba. In exchange, the U.S. publicly agreed not to invade Cuba and secretly agreed to remove its own missiles from Turkey, which were pointed at the Soviet Union.

The resolution of the Cuban Missile Crisis is widely regarded as a testament to the power of thoughtful action and restraint. Kennedy's decision to avoid immediate military confrontation, combined with his efforts to engage in diplomacy, averted a potential nuclear disaster. The crisis underscored the importance of careful decision-making and the value of seeking peaceful solutions even in the most tense and dangerous situations.

The Cuban Missile Crisis had a lasting impact on the U.S.-Soviet relations and on global diplomacy. It led to increased efforts to establish communication channels and crisis management mechanisms between the superpowers. The establishment of the "hotline" between Washington and Moscow and the subsequent arms control agreements were direct outcomes of the lessons learned during the crisis.

In summary, the Cuban Missile Crisis is a powerful example of how careful reflection and measured action can prevent catastrophic outcomes. President Kennedy's decision to opt for a naval blockade and engage in diplomatic negotiations, rather than immediate military action, played a crucial role in averting a nuclear conflict. The crisis remains a poignant reminder of the importance of thoughtful leadership in maintaining global peace and stability.

Hasty actions disrupt peace; thoughtful actions preserve it. Take time to reflect before you act, ensuring that your decisions align with your values and long-term goals.
It is never a good thing to make decisions in a haste. Most decisions which are made in haste often lead to tears, regret and frustration. It is wisdom to take time to reflect before you act. A wise man will make sure he crosses his "T" and dot his "i" before making a decision.

Hasty actions disrupt peace while thoughtful action preserves it. You will notice that you often regret the actions you take on impulse and find peace in actions you took after reflecting. Acting on impulse often leads to regret, conflicted emotions, inner conflict, damaged relationships and reputations, lost growth and missed opportunities.

Reflecting is very important and is beneficial for you. When you reflect before acting, you clarify your thoughts, help you align your decisions with your values and goals, reduce your stress and anxiety and increase your confidence and self-trust. Reflecting is a powerful tool for making thoughtful decisions. If Ted had reflected and taken his time before investing his money into the business Jon introduced him to, he would not have fallen for the scam. By reflecting, you build inner wisdom and reduce your stress and anxiety.

When reflecting, take time to calm your mind and emotions, ask yourself questions, "what are my motivations?", "What are the potential consequences of taking this action?". Look at the situation from a different perspective and ensure that your decision aligns with what is important to you. Always take a moment to reflect and find peace in your decision.

Law 11

RELEASE ATTACHMENT TO OUTCOMES

"The only way to peace is to let go of the desire for specific results." — Epictetus

Thomas Edison, one of history's most renowned inventors, is best known for his pivotal role in developing the incandescent lightbulb. However, this achievement was not the result of a straightforward path to success but rather a long and arduous journey marked by numerous setbacks and relentless experimentation. Edison's story serves as a profound illustration of how perseverance and a focus on the process, rather than solely on the end result, can lead to groundbreaking innovation.

In the late 19th century, Edison set out to create a practical and long-lasting electric light source. At the time, electric lighting was in its infancy, and existing solutions were either too short-lived or impractical for widespread use. Edison's goal was to develop an incandescent lightbulb that could provide a reliable, sustainable glow suitable for everyday use. This quest was fraught with technical challenges, particularly in finding a suitable filament material that could withstand the electric current and provide consistent illumination.

Edison's approach to solving this problem was methodical and unyielding. He embarked on an exhaustive process of experimentation, testing over a thousand different materials in his search for the perfect filament. These materials ranged from carbonized paper and bamboo to various metal alloys. Despite his best efforts, many of these materials either burned out quickly or did not produce sufficient light.

Edison's determination in the face of these failures was remarkable. Each trial that failed to meet his criteria was not viewed as a defeat but as a valuable learning opportunity. Edison famously remarked, "I have not failed. I've just found 10,000 ways that won't work." This mindset reflects a deep understanding of the importance of learning from setbacks and maintaining focus on the iterative process of innovation.

Edison meticulously documented each experiment, noting the characteristics and shortcomings of each material tested. His methodical approach allowed him to analyze what did not work and to adjust his strategy accordingly. This rigorous documentation and iterative process were crucial in refining his approach and eventually identifying viable solutions.

After years of relentless experimentation, Edison and his team discovered that a carbon filament, derived from bamboo, could sustain a glowing light for extended periods. This breakthrough was achieved through a combination of persistence, meticulous research, and an unwavering commitment to the process. Edison's carbon filament provided the foundation for the incandescent lightbulb, a revolutionary invention that transformed the way the world used light.

The practical success of Edison's lightbulb marked a turning point in technological advancement, leading to the widespread adoption of electric lighting. The impact of this invention was profound, influencing the development of modern electrical systems and changing daily life in countless ways.

Edison's journey to inventing the lightbulb offers several key lessons:

1. **Perseverance:** Edison's ability to persist through numerous failures exemplifies the value of perseverance in the face of adversity. His story illustrates that innovation often requires overcoming repeated setbacks and maintaining dedication to the goal.

2. **Learning from Failure:** Edison's perspective on failure as a learning experience highlights the importance of viewing setbacks as opportunities for growth. Each failed attempt provided critical insights that ultimately led to success.

3. **Focus on Process:** Edison's emphasis on the process rather than solely on the outcome underscores a broader lesson in

innovation. By concentrating on the iterative nature of experimentation and adjusting based on what was learned, Edison was able to achieve his goal.

4. **Impact of Innovation:** The successful development of the incandescent lightbulb had far-reaching effects, demonstrating how perseverance and dedication to problem-solving can lead to significant advancements that shape the future.

In summary, Thomas Edison's path to inventing the lightbulb exemplifies the power of perseverance, the importance of learning from failures, and the value of focusing on the process of innovation. His relentless pursuit and methodical approach not only led to a groundbreaking invention but also provided a lasting legacy that continues to inspire and inform the pursuit of scientific and technological progress.

Clinging to specific outcomes breeds anxiety. Instead, focus on your efforts and let the results unfold as they will. Peace is found in detachment, knowing you have done your best. It will do you no good to worry over what you have no control over. We all want specific results from our lives but it will be futile to obsess over the results we hope to achieve. The best thing you can do is to focus on putting in the work and allow the outcome to unfold naturally.

When you hold onto specific outcomes, you may experience disappointment, frustration, fear of failure, anxiety, stress, perfectionism, missed opportunities and growth. Whenever your expectations are not met, you will become dejected, sad and depressed.

Attachment to outcomes stems from your desire for security and control. Your belief that your happiness, validation, and sense of accomplishment comes from achieving specific results causes you to get attached to specific outcomes. Whenever these outcomes are not achieved, you will suffer the risk of facing disappointment, anxiety and stress.

When you are fixed on a particular result or outcome, you risk limiting your potential. You may miss out on other opportunities and experiences when your mind is set on a particular result. You also set yourself up for disappointment, get overly attached to a particular outcome that you become resistant to change or feedback.

Detaching yourself from specific outcomes allows you to concentrate on what you can control, build awareness and stay present instead of worrying about the future. When you are detached from specific outcomes, you will build resilience from learning to adapt and grow from unexpected outcomes. You also learn to treat yourself with kindness regardless of the outcome.

Instead of setting specific outcomes for yourself, set intentions. Focus on making progress not perfection. Do not make decisions based on a specific outcome, instead make decisions based on your values and principles. Build connections with people rather than be obsessed with specific results. You should learn to embrace learning from opportunities and challenges regardless of the outcome.

Law 12

KEEP YOUR EXPECTATIONS IN CHECK

"The key to peace is lowering expectations and embracing reality." - Epictetus

Helen Keller's extraordinary journey from darkness and silence to global prominence serves as a powerful testament to the value of managing expectations and embracing one's unique path. Born in 1880 in Tuscumbia, Alabama, Keller's life took a dramatic turn when she was struck by an illness, possibly scarlet fever or meningitis, at just 19 months old. This illness left her both deaf and blind, plunging her into a world of darkness and silence.

Keller's early years were marked by significant challenges. Her inability to communicate with those around her led to profound frustration and isolation. Her parents, though deeply committed to her well-being, struggled to find effective methods for teaching and interacting with her. Traditional educational approaches proved inadequate for addressing her unique needs, and Keller's isolation grew as she grappled with a sense of being cut off from the world.

The transformative moment in Keller's life came with the arrival of Anne Sullivan, a teacher from the Perkins Institute for the Blind. Sullivan, who herself had faced significant hardships, brought a profound understanding of the challenges of blindness and deafness. She approached Keller with remarkable patience and determination, beginning her work by using sign language to bridge the communication gap.

Sullivan's approach was grounded in setting realistic and achievable goals. She understood that conventional methods of education were not suited for Keller's situation and instead focused on her unique abilities and interests. This personalized approach was pivotal in breaking through the barriers of Keller's isolation.

One of the most memorable and profound milestones in Keller's education was her breakthrough moment with the word "water." Sullivan used tactile sign language to spell out the word on Keller's hand while running water over it. This moment was a breakthrough in Keller's understanding of language, representing more than just a new word—it was a gateway to a world of communication and learning. Sullivan and Keller celebrated each small victory, recognizing them as significant achievements in their own right.

As Keller grew older, her accomplishments continued to defy

expectations. She became a passionate advocate for people with disabilities, using her experiences to highlight the importance of empathy, understanding, and accessible education. Her advocacy extended beyond her own circumstances, aiming to improve the lives of others facing similar challenges.

In 1904, Keller achieved another monumental milestone by graduating from Radcliffe College, becoming the first deaf-blind person to earn a Bachelor of Arts degree. Her academic success was a testament to her relentless determination and the effective guidance of Sullivan. Keller's achievements in education and advocacy demonstrated that limitations could be transcended through perseverance and realistic goal-setting.

Helen Keller's story is a profound reminder of the power of managing expectations and focusing on progress rather than perfection. Her journey from a state of profound isolation to becoming a renowned advocate and scholar underscores several key lessons:

1. Realistic Goal-Setting: Keller's and Sullivan's approach to education was based on setting achievable goals tailored to Keller's abilities. This method allowed Keller to build on small successes, gradually achieving greater milestones.

2. Embracing Circumstances: Keller's acceptance of her situation, combined with Sullivan's innovative teaching methods, enabled her to leverage her unique abilities rather than

be defined by her limitations.

3. Celebrating Progress: By recognizing and celebrating each small victory, Keller and Sullivan fostered a positive and motivating environment. This approach helped Keller build confidence and resilience.

4. Advocacy and Inspiration: Keller's later work as an advocate for disability rights and her academic success provided a powerful example of how determination and realistic expectations can lead to extraordinary achievements.

Helen Keller's journey is a testament to how managing expectations and focusing on incremental progress can lead to remarkable accomplishments. Her story illustrates the transformative power of patience, perseverance, and a supportive approach to education and personal growth. Keller's legacy continues to inspire and remind us that limitations can be overcome with determination, empathy, and a commitment to embracing one's unique path.

Unmet expectations lead to disappointment and unrest. Lower your expectations of others and the world, and you will find peace in the absence of constant disillusionment. Did you know that you can only be disappointed by someone you had expectations from? If you have no expectations from a thing or a person, you can not be disappointed in them because there is nothing to be disappointed in.

You will be frustrated, angry and disappointed if you expected a friend or relative to behave in a particular way but they didn't. It is important that you learn to keep your expectations in check. Lowered expectations always leads to a more peaceful life.

Many relationships were strained and had major conflict because one party had an expectation from the other party that was not met. You will always be frustrated and angry if you don't lower your expectations. Know that expectations can be cut short and there is nothing you can do about it. It is futile to worry about things that are beyond your control. Give allowances for people to go or do below what you expected.

It is wrong to think that people or things will behave or work in a particular way. People cannot be predicted. You cannot control how others behave or what an outcome will be, let things follow their natural course without interfering. When you set unrealistic standards for yourself and others, you set yourself up for frustration.

It is important that we learn how to lower our expectations or check them in check, if we want to enjoy peace with ourselves and others. To lower your expectations, you need to understand that people and situations are imperfect and let go of unrealistic expectations about others and outcomes. You should also learn that others have their own struggles and limitations. These will help you to check your expectations.

Law 13

PRACTICE FORGIVENESS

"Forgiveness is the final form of love." - Reinhold Niebuhr

Desmond Tutu, an influential South African bishop and fervent anti-apartheid activist, is renowned for his profound commitment to forgiveness and reconciliation. His leadership during a pivotal period in South Africa's history underscores the transformative power of these principles in addressing profound injustice and fostering national healing.

South Africa's apartheid era was characterized by severe racial segregation and institutionalized violence, leaving a legacy of deep-seated trauma and division. The system of apartheid, which enforced racial discrimination and inequality, led to countless human rights abuses and atrocities. As the country approached the end of apartheid in the early 1990s, there was a pressing need to address the wounds of the past and find a way to reconcile a divided society.

In 1995, Desmond Tutu was appointed chair of the Truth and Reconciliation Commission (TRC), a body established to uncover the truth about human rights violations committed during the apartheid era and to promote healing and reconciliation. The TRC was a unique and ambitious initiative designed to provide a platform for victims to share their stories, for perpetrators to confess their crimes, and for the nation to confront its troubled history.

Tutu's approach to the TRC was deeply influenced by his Christian beliefs and his understanding of forgiveness as a cornerstone of personal and national healing. He advocated for a process that focused not on retribution but on understanding and reconciliation. Tutu famously declared, "Without forgiveness, there is no future." This statement encapsulated his belief that forgiveness was essential for the healing of individuals and for the nation's ability to move forward from the shadows of apartheid.

The TRC hearings were a powerful and emotional process. Victims of apartheid-era violence were given the opportunity to recount their suffering, often in the presence of the perpetrators who had wronged them. This public and transparent process was intended to acknowledge the pain inflicted and to begin the healing process.

One of the most poignant moments occurred during the hearings when a former soldier, who had committed severe acts of violence against anti-apartheid activists, testified before the commission. Desmond Tutu, instead of expressing condemnation, responded with compassion and empathy. He recognized the complexity of human behavior and the deep psychological and societal factors that contributed to the actions of the perpetrator. This response highlighted Tutu's commitment to understanding the broader context of the conflict and the need for healing on both sides of the divide.

Under Tutu's leadership, the TRC facilitated a national conversation about the atrocities of apartheid and the path to reconciliation. The commission's work helped South Africa confront its past in a way that allowed for a collective understanding of the injustices suffered and a way forward that was rooted in forgiveness rather than vengeance.

The TRC's approach, guided by Tutu's philosophy, enabled South Africa to make a crucial transition from a period of systemic oppression to a more inclusive and democratic society. The process was not without its challenges and criticisms, but it represented a significant attempt to address the deep wounds inflicted by decades of apartheid.

Desmond Tutu's legacy is a powerful reminder of the transformative potential of forgiveness and reconciliation. His leadership demonstrated that facing the past with compassion and understanding can pave the way for personal and collective peace. Tutu's contributions have had a lasting impact, not only on South Africa but on the broader global discourse about conflict resolution and healing.

Desmond Tutu's work with the Truth and Reconciliation Commission exemplifies how forgiveness and reconciliation can play a pivotal role in overcoming the legacies of injustice and division. His emphasis on compassion, understanding, and the acknowledgment of both victim and perpetrator perspectives was instrumental in helping South Africa navigate a complex transition and build a foundation for a more unified future. Tutu's approach to managing the profound injustices of apartheid through forgiveness continues to inspire and remind us of the power of empathy and reconciliation in achieving lasting peace.

Holding onto grudges is like carrying a heavy burden. Release yourself from the weight of past wrongs by practicing forgiveness. Peace flows from a heart unburdened by resentment.

If you are looking to enjoy personal growth, healing and transformation, be quick to forgive. When we forgive, we release ourselves from resentment, anger and bitterness. Resentment, anger and unforgiveness can consume us, affect our relationships, mental health and our overall well being.

Forgiveness is liberating; it releases you from the weight of unforgiveness. You can liken resentment to carrying a heavy weight that is weighing you down and preventing you from moving forward. Resentment can lead to feeling drained, hopeless and exhausted. You may begin to experience emotional pain, depression and anxiety. The weight of resentment can damage your connection with others and lead to tension and disease.

The following are the root of resentment;

- Unmet expectations, disappointments and betrayals can lead to resentment.

- Feeling injustice; when you are wronged, treated unfair or unequally.

- Resentment can stem from fear of vulnerability, rejection and abandonment.

- When you fail to self-reflect, you may become resentful.

Forgiveness does not happen in a day, it is a process. It is a journey towards release, growth and healing. It helps us to release emotional burdens that come from resentment. When we forgive, we mend, recover and move forward. Forgiveness offers us a chance to rebuild connection, trust and restore relationships. Ultimately, forgiveness helps us to achieve serenity, contentment and nurture our inner peace.

There are practical steps you can follow to forgive and they include;

- Acknowledge how you feel, the pain, anger and hurt, don't lie to yourself.

- Don't think of taking revenge or to pay back. Let bygones be bygones.

- Remember that we are all humans and we can make mistakes and make rash decisions.

- Learn and grow from the experience.

- Seek support if you need to. You don't have to journey alone. --Forgiveness is not a day's journey and it does not mean you should condone or forget what has happened. It means releasing the burden of the past wrongs and hurts.

Law 14

ESTABLISH
BOUNDARIES

"The boundaries we set determine the quality of our peace." - Epictetus

E leanor Roosevelt, First Lady of the United States from 1933 to 1945, is celebrated not only for her role in supporting her husband, President Franklin D. Roosevelt, but also for her groundbreaking work in human rights and social justice. Her life and career demonstrate the power of establishing personal and public boundaries to pursue one's principles and advocate for those who lack a voice.

Eleanor Roosevelt's marriage to Franklin D. Roosevelt was a partnership marked by both collaboration and personal challenge. Franklin's political ambitions and the demands of his role often took him away from the personal sphere, allowing Eleanor to carve out her own space. Despite the constraints imposed by traditional gender roles of her time, Eleanor resolutely defined her own identity, focusing on issues that mattered to her and refusing to be confined by societal expectations.

She faced significant challenges in balancing her roles as a wife, mother, and public figure. Her work required her to navigate the complexities of her husband's political career while also confronting the prejudices and limitations imposed on women in public life. Eleanor set firm boundaries around her principles, ensuring that her advocacy for social justice and human rights remained a central focus of her life.

In the aftermath of World War II, Eleanor Roosevelt emerged as a leading figure in the international effort to establish human rights standards. Her involvement in the drafting of the Universal Declaration of Human Rights in 1948 was a testament to her unwavering commitment to justice and equality. Despite facing opposition from various political figures and organizations, Roosevelt remained resolute in her vision for a just world.

Her role in the drafting process was both influential and challenging. She worked tirelessly to articulate and champion a comprehensive vision for human rights, reflecting her belief in the inherent dignity and rights of all individuals. Roosevelt's leadership in this endeavor was instrumental in shaping a document that would become a cornerstone of international human rights law.

Eleanor Roosevelt's advocacy extended beyond the drafting of the Universal Declaration of Human Rights. She actively promoted social justice and human rights throughout her life, addressing issues such as racial segregation, women's rights, and labor conditions. Her work helped lay the groundwork for future human rights initiatives and inspired countless individuals to engage in advocacy and social reform.

Roosevelt's ability to set and maintain boundaries was crucial to her success. By clearly defining her values and prioritizing her principles, she managed to balance her various roles and responsibilities while remaining true to her commitment to social justice. Her legacy teaches us that establishing boundaries is essential for personal peace and effective advocacy.

Eleanor Roosevelt's contributions to human rights and social justice had a profound and lasting impact. The Universal Declaration of Human Rights, shaped by her vision and determination, continues to serve as a vital framework for international human rights standards. Her work inspired future generations to advocate for justice and equality, and her example remains a powerful reminder of the importance of maintaining one's principles in the face of challenges.

Her legacy is also evident in the continued relevance of her work in advancing social justice. Eleanor Roosevelt's commitment to addressing the needs of the marginalized and underserved helped drive significant social change, and her influence is still felt in contemporary human rights discourse.

Eleanor Roosevelt's life and work exemplify the power of setting boundaries to maintain personal integrity and pursue meaningful change. Her steadfast commitment to human rights and social justice, coupled with her ability to balance her personal and public roles, left a lasting legacy that continues to inspire and inform the pursuit of equality and justice. Roosevelt's story teaches us that by defining our principles and focusing on our values, we can achieve profound impact and contribute to a more just and equitable world.

Peace is maintained by clear boundaries. Know your limits and enforce them with kindness but firmness. Do not allow others to encroach upon your peace by overstepping their bounds. Learn to say no! Saying no does not mean you are evil or inconsiderate. It means you know what you are doing and you can stand for yourself. If you don't know how to set clear boundaries, people will encroach on your time, energy, and emotional space. Don't be afraid of saying no because of fear of rejection, conflict or disappointment. Know that you cannot always satisfy people, if you will maintain peace you must be able to set boundaries.

Boundaries are very important, they are the foundation for healthy relationships, self care and emotional resilience. When you set clear boundaries, you protect your time, energy, resources, and emotional well being. You promote mutual respect and understanding and encourage healthy communication.

To set clear boundaries, you must first identify and recognize your limit. Ask yourself questions such as;

- What drains and stresses me?

- What are my values and priorities?

- What are my non-negotiables?

Setting boundaries doesn't have to be aggressive or confrontational. You can say "No" with kindness and firmness. Express your feelings and needs using "I", be direct, clear and specific and offer alternatives or solutions when possible. When establishing your boundaries, start small and work your way up. Speak confidently and respectfully. It is also important to set your boundaries early and consistently reinforce your boundaries. Ensure that you prioritize yourself; you matter.

When you learn to set clear boundaries and say "No" with kindness and firmness, you will protect your space and create a peaceful and balanced life for yourself.

Law 15

HARMONIZE WITH NATURE

"Nature does not hurry, yet everything is accomplished." - Lao Tzu

John Muir, often celebrated as the "Father of the National Parks," was a pioneering naturalist and environmentalist whose profound connection to nature significantly shaped American conservation efforts during the late 19th and early 20th centuries. His deep appreciation for the wilderness and his commitment to preserving natural landscapes have left an indelible mark on environmentalism.

John Muir was born in 1838 in Scotland. His family emigrated to the United States when he was a child, settling in Wisconsin. The move to the American wilderness ignited Muir's lifelong passion for nature. As a young man, Muir explored the forests and meadows around his new home, developing a profound appreciation for the natural world.

His early experiences in nature were formative, and he soon began to see the wilderness as not just a physical space but as a vital, living entity with which humans should live in harmony.

Muir's philosophy centered on the belief that the health of the planet was intrinsically linked to human well-being. This understanding would become a driving force behind his conservation efforts.

In 1868, Muir embarked on a transformative journey to the Sierra Nevada mountains in California, a region that would become central to his environmental advocacy. His experiences in the Sierra Nevada, including the awe-inspiring beauty of Yosemite Valley, deeply influenced his views on conservation. Muir's observations of the natural world were not just scientific but also philosophical, reflecting his belief in the interconnectedness of all life.

Muir's adventures in the wilderness were more than just explorations; they were profound experiences that deepened his commitment to preserving natural landscapes. He spent years studying and writing about the Sierra Nevada, capturing its splendor and the urgent need to protect it. In 1892, Muir co-founded the Sierra Club, an organization dedicated to environmental conservation and the preservation of natural areas. The Sierra Club played a crucial role in advocating for the establishment of national parks and the protection of natural landscapes. Under Muir's leadership, the club worked tirelessly to promote conservation policies and to raise public awareness about the importance of preserving wilderness areas.

One of the Sierra Club's early successes was the campaign to establish Yosemite National Park as a protected area. Muir's tireless efforts, combined with the advocacy of the Sierra Club, led to the park's designation as a national park in 1890. This achievement marked a significant milestone in the American conservation movement and set a precedent for the creation of future national parks.

Muir's philosophy of living in harmony with nature was deeply rooted in his belief that human well-being is intimately connected to the health of the natural world. His famous quote, "In every walk with nature one receives far more than he seeks," reflects his understanding that engaging with the natural world offers profound personal fulfillment and a sense of peace.

Muir's legacy is not only evident in the national parks he helped establish but also in the broader environmental movement he inspired. His writings continue to resonate with those who seek to understand and appreciate the beauty of the natural world. The Sierra Club, which remains a leading environmental organization, continues to advocate for conservation and environmental stewardship in line with Muir's vision. Muir's emphasis on the spiritual and emotional benefits of connecting with nature has influenced countless individuals and movements dedicated to environmental conservation.

Muir's life exemplifies how a deep, personal connection to nature can drive meaningful change. His ability to articulate the beauty and importance of the natural world through his writings and advocacy has inspired a global appreciation for environmental stewardship. John Muir's dedication to harmonizing with nature and his efforts to preserve natural landscapes have left a lasting legacy. His work not only contributed to the establishment of national parks but also inspired a broader movement towards environmental conservation. Muir's life and philosophy teach us the value of connecting with the natural world and the profound peace that comes from living in harmony with it. His legacy continues to inspire environmentalists and nature enthusiasts worldwide, reminding us of the importance of preserving the natural beauty of our planet for future generations.

Align yourself with the rhythms of nature. Rise and rest with the sun, eat foods that nourish your body, and spend time in the natural world. Nature is a wellspring of peace for those who seek it. Our world today is a fast paced one, with almost everybody working a "9 to 5" and others working round the clock, we easily get cut up in the hustle and bustle of daily life. We forget to connect with the natural world, take a stroll and eat fresh food.

You are likely to notice a reduction in your stress and anxiety level, improved sleep, increased sense of belonging and connection, boosted moods and energy levels, and heightened sense of mindfulness when you harmonize with nature.

Did you know that aligning your sleep schedule with the Sun's rhythm is good for you? This will regulate your circadian rhythms and improve your sleep. Although canned foods are fast to prepare, they are very good for your health. Find time to nourish your body with locally sourced food. If you work remotely, schedule a 30 minutes outdoor time per day for yourself. Take a walk in the park, go hiking or visit a friend's garden. Spend time appreciating the sights, smells, sounds and texture of nature. The truth is we don't do this enough. We are often overwhelmed with our daily struggles that we overlook nature. Take a break from your screen. You can decide to do a technology-free weekend or digital detox. This will help reduce stress and increase your connection with nature. If you are not used to spending time in nature, start small, then gradually increase it. Incorporate nature visit into your daily routine, you can go with your friends or family.

Law 16

PRACTICE COMPASSION

"Compassion is the ultimate expression of humanity." - Chenrezig

Mother Teresa, born in Albania in 1910 as Agnes Gonxha Bojaxhiu, dedicated her life to serving the poorest of the poor in Calcutta, India. In 1948, she felt called to leave her teaching position and devote herself entirely to helping the destitute. She founded the Missionaries of Charity, an organization committed to caring for those who were sick, homeless, and abandoned. Her deep compassion for the suffering became her guiding principle, leading her to embrace the most marginalized members of society.

Mother Teresa often spoke about the importance of seeing Christ in every person, stating, "Each one of them is Jesus in disguise." This perspective allowed her to approach her work with genuine empathy and love. She established numerous homes and clinics, providing food, medical care, and shelter to those in need. Her work extended beyond mere charity; she aimed to restore dignity and hope to those often overlooked by society.

In 1979, she received the Nobel Peace Prize for her humanitarian efforts, yet she remained humble, emphasizing that her mission was about service, not recognition. Mother Teresa's life teaches us that practicing compassion not only brings peace to others but also fosters a profound sense of fulfillment within ourselves. Her legacy continues to inspire individuals worldwide to engage in acts of kindness and service, highlighting the transformative power of compassion.

Compassion for others is a pathway to inner peace. When you act with kindness and empathy, you create a ripple of peace that spreads beyond yourself. Being compassionate can lead you to a more fulfilling and peaceful life. Compassion is more than feeling sorry for others, it is the ability to connect with others on a deep level, understanding their struggles and pain and offering them kindness and support. It has to do with putting yourself in other's shoes. Compassion does not just end with the person who was shown compassion. It creates a ripple effect. Your acts of kindness and empathy can touch the lives around you.

When we focus on helping others, we shift our attention away from our worries, concerns and struggles which allows us to let go of every negative emotion and thought. Practicing compassion helps us to offer kindness and support to those around us, volunteer our time and energy to help those in need and build a deeper understanding of yourself and others. When we choose to see the world through the eyes of others, to understand their struggles and share their burdens, we create a more harmonious and peaceful world. And in doing so, we find peace within ourselves.

We live in a world that values results and achievements over people and relationships, which makes it difficult to put others' needs before us. You will need to be deliberate and intentional to be compassionate, kind and loving. Make a conscious effort to practice compassion and see as it impacts your life and the lives of those around you.

Law 17

LET GO OF EGO

"The ego is the root of much discord." - Epictetus

P resident Abraham Lincoln, often celebrated as one of America's most revered leaders, exemplified the principle of letting go of ego throughout his presidency. His leadership during the American Civil War demonstrated a profound commitment to humility, integrity, and the pursuit of the greater good over personal ambition.

Lincoln's presidency was marked by unprecedented challenges, including a nation torn apart by civil war, deep political divisions, and social upheaval. Leading the country through such tumultuous times required not only strategic acumen but also a personal fortitude and humility that allowed him to navigate complex and often contentious issues. One of Lincoln's most notable strategies was his decision to form a diverse group of advisors, known as his "Team of Rivals." Rather than surrounding himself with individuals who merely echoed his own views, Lincoln deliberately chose advisors with differing perspectives. This approach included political opponents such as William H. Seward, Salmon P. Chase, and Edward Bates, who had once contested for the Republican presidential nomination.

Lincoln's choice to include these rivals in his cabinet was driven by his belief in the importance of a broad and inclusive approach to governance. He valued their expertise and perspectives, recognizing that a variety of viewpoints could contribute to more balanced and informed decision-making. This willingness to embrace dissent and seek counsel from a range of advisors was a testament to his humility and his commitment to the nation's welfare over personal pride.

One of Lincoln's most significant achievements, the Emancipation Proclamation, exemplifies his approach to leadership and humility. When drafting the Proclamation, Lincoln engaged with both abolitionists, who were pushing for the end of slavery, and military leaders, who were concerned with the practical implications of such a measure. He understood the necessity of a unified strategy to address the deeply divided nation.

Lincoln's decision to issue the Proclamation was not made lightly. He grappled with its potential impact on the war effort and the Union's future. His consultations with various stakeholders demonstrated his commitment to making a decision that balanced moral imperatives with practical realities. The Proclamation, which declared the freedom of enslaved individuals in Confederate-held territories, was a crucial step towards the abolition of slavery and reflected

Lincoln's dedication to justice and equality.

Lincoln's humility extended beyond his interactions with his advisors and into his public persona. He was known for his straightforward and unpretentious demeanor, which earned him respect and trust from both allies and opponents. His famous quote, "I am not bound to win, but I am bound to be true," encapsulated his dedication to integrity over personal success.

In his speeches and policies, Lincoln prioritized the nation's needs and values over his own ego or political gain. This commitment to truth and principle guided him through the difficult decisions of his presidency and contributed to his enduring legacy.

Abraham Lincoln's presidency is often celebrated for its remarkable leadership and moral courage. His ability to let go of ego, seek diverse perspectives, and prioritize the nation's well-being over personal ambition was instrumental in navigating the complexities of the Civil War. Lincoln's humility and dedication to integrity helped him make difficult decisions that ultimately led to the preservation of the Union and the advancement of human rights.

Lincoln's legacy serves as a powerful reminder of the impact that humility and selflessness can have on effective leadership. Abraham Lincoln's presidency is a profound example of how letting go of ego and embracing humility can lead to transformative leadership. His approach to governance, characterized by a willingness to listen to differing opinions and prioritize the nation's needs, contributed to his success in leading the country through one of its most challenging periods. Lincoln's legacy endures as a testament to the power of integrity and the importance of placing principle over personal ambition.

The ego is the root of much discord. To find peace, let go of your need for recognition and superiority. Embrace humility and recognize your place within the greater whole. If you always crave for validation and recognition from others, if you feel superior as if you are in a competition with those around, then you have what is called Ego. Ego can be a very powerful force in our lives, driving us to seek validation and making us feel disconnected from others and ourselves. People who are driven by their ego focus on their needs and desires at the expense of others. Everything is about them, which leads to feeling separate, competing and fighting with others. Rather than recognizing what we have in common, we will begin to see ourselves as superior or inferior.

One of the signs that shows that a person has ego is the constant need for recognition. The need for recognition can be a heavy burden to carry. It leaves you strained, anxious and insecure. We may become like a bottomless pit, that always seeks more but never finds peace. To break free from ego, you must learn to be humble. Humility helps us to see ourselves as part of a larger humanity that is totally dependent on each other.

Listening to yourself speaking, embracing your mistakes and vulnerabilities and recognizing the achievements and contribution of others are the few ways you can practice humility among others. Like Epictetus said, the ego is the root of much discord. By letting go of our need for recognition and superiority, we can find peace and live in harmony with others. Letting go of your ego is a process, it takes time, practice and patience. Your life will be filled with peace, fulfillment and connections when you let go. Living a life that reflects your deepest values and aspirations, letting go of validation and the weight of ego can help you experience peace and fulfillment on a deeper level.

Law 18

PRACTICE REGULAR CONTEMPLATION

"The mind is everything; what you think, you become." - Buddha

Socrates, one of the most influential philosophers in Western history, lived in Athens during the 5th century BCE and profoundly shaped the intellectual landscape of his time. His commitment to self-reflection and philosophical inquiry not only established the foundation for Western philosophy but also illustrated the transformative power of contemplation.

Socrates is best known for his method of inquiry, commonly referred to as the Socratic Method. This approach involved engaging in dialogue with others to stimulate critical thinking and expose underlying assumptions. Socrates would often initiate conversations in the bustling streets of Athens, asking probing questions about concepts such as justice, virtue, and knowledge.

His method was less about providing answers and more about

encouraging others to think deeply about their beliefs. Through a series of questions and answers, Socrates aimed to lead his interlocutors to recognize contradictions in their thinking and to clarify their understanding. This technique fostered a culture of self-examination and intellectual rigor, challenging individuals to scrutinize their values and ethical principles.

Socrates famously declared, "The unexamined life is not worth living," highlighting his belief that contemplation and self-reflection are essential to a meaningful and fulfilling life. For Socrates, the pursuit of self-knowledge and understanding was paramount. He believed that only through rigorous self-examination could individuals achieve true wisdom and live a life of integrity.

This principle guided his actions and interactions. Socrates placed great emphasis on introspection as a means to personal and moral development. He encouraged others to question their assumptions and to seek deeper insights into their own lives and the world around them.

Socrates' commitment to his philosophical principles was put to the ultimate test in 399 BCE when he was put on trial in Athens. He faced charges of impiety and corrupting the youth, accusations that stemmed from his unconventional ideas and critical questioning of Athenian norms.

Despite the gravity of the situation, Socrates approached his trial with characteristic calmness and composure. He chose to defend his actions and beliefs rather than flee or recant. Socrates viewed the trial as an opportunity to further explore and discuss philosophical concepts such as justice, virtue, and the role of the philosopher in society.

During the trial, Socrates continued to engage in dialogue, challenging the court's assumptions and defending his method of inquiry. His ability to maintain his philosophical integrity in the face of adversity exemplified his deep commitment to the principles of contemplation and self-examination.

Socrates' approach to philosophy and his unwavering dedication to contemplation have left a lasting impact on Western thought. His emphasis on self-examination and critical inquiry laid the groundwork for subsequent philosophical traditions and ethical theories. Socrates' influence is particularly evident in the works of his students, such as Plato, who preserved and expanded upon his ideas.

Socrates' legacy endures in the belief that thoughtful reflection and the pursuit of self-knowledge are crucial to personal growth and understanding. His life and teachings continue to inspire individuals to engage in introspection, challenge their assumptions, and seek deeper wisdom.

Socrates' dedication to contemplation and philosophical inquiry exemplifies the transformative power of self-examination. His use of the Socratic Method to stimulate critical thinking, coupled with his commitment to facing adversity with integrity, highlights the profound impact of contemplation on personal and intellectual development. Socrates' legacy serves as a powerful reminder of the importance of examining one's life and beliefs, demonstrating that true wisdom and fulfillment come from a relentless quest for self-knowledge.

Our minds are always working and it can be quite difficult to find a moment of peace, regular contemplation can help you to build inner peace and calm. Set aside time each day for quiet contemplation. Whether through meditation, prayer, or reflection, this practice will center your mind and nourish your spirit, fostering peace within.

Contemplation is the practice of taking time to quiet the mind and focus on the present moment. It's about creating space for reflection, introspection, and connection with your inner self. Contemplation can take many forms, including meditation, prayer, journaling, or simply taking a few deep breaths.

We live in a world where we are constantly connected to our devices, social media, and the news. This can lead to feelings of overwhelm, anxiety, and stress. Contemplation provides a much needed respite from the chaos, allowing us to:

- Calm the mind and reduce stress

- Increase self-awareness and introspection

- Connect with our values and purpose

- Cultivate gratitude and appreciation

- Improve focus and concentration

You can practice contemplation by following the steps below.
- Start small: Begin with just 5-10 minutes a day and gradually increase as you become more comfortable with the practice.

- Find a quiet space: Identify a quiet, comfortable spot where you can sit and reflect without distractions.

- Focus on your breath: Bring your attention to your breath, noticing the sensation of the air moving in and out of your body.

- Let go of distractions: Gently let go of thoughts and distractions, returning your focus to the present moment.

- Be consistent: Make contemplation a daily habit, ideally at the same time each day.

There are several forms of contemplation to explore, which includes meditation; focusing on the breath, a mantra, or a visualization to quiet the mind, prayer; connecting with a higher power or the universe, expressing gratitude and intention and journaling; writing down your thoughts, feelings, and insights to process and reflect.

Peace and wisdom arise from the depths of our own minds. Difficulty quieting the mind, feeling restless or uncomfortable, and struggling to make time can hinder contemplation. Regular contemplation is a simple yet powerful practice that can help you cultivate inner peace and calm. As Epictetus taught, contemplation centers our minds, nourishes our spirits, and fosters inner peace.

Law 19

ACCEPT IMPERMANENCE

"Nothing is permanent except change." –
Heraclitus **Siddhartha Gautama:

The Buddha's Journey to Enlightenment and the Teachings on Impermanence**
Siddhartha Gautama, who would come to be known as the Buddha, is one of the most influential figures in spiritual history. Living in the 5th century BCE, he founded Buddhism, a major world religion that offers profound insights into the nature of existence and the path to inner peace. Central to his teachings is the concept of impermanence, or "anicca" in Pali, which he explored deeply through his own life experiences and meditative practice.

Born into a life of luxury as a prince in the Shakya kingdom, Siddhartha Gautama was initially shielded from the harsh realities of life. His father, King Suddhodana, had ensured that Siddhartha lived a life of comfort, with every conceivable pleasure at his disposal. However, despite this opulent existence, Siddhartha's encounters with the impermanent nature of life would profoundly alter his path.

The turning point came when Siddhartha ventured beyond the palace grounds and encountered the stark realities of aging, illness, and death. Witnessing these forms of suffering for the first time, Siddhartha was struck by the realization that all things, including his own life and the world around him, were subject to change and decay. This insight shattered his previously held beliefs and prompted a deep existential crisis.

Determined to seek answers to the fundamental questions about human suffering, Siddhartha renounced his princely life and embarked on a journey of spiritual quest. He adopted the life of an ascetic, dedicating himself to rigorous meditation and contemplation. Siddhartha explored various spiritual practices and philosophies, searching for a way to overcome suffering and achieve lasting peace.

After years of intense practice and self-discipline, Siddhartha's search led him to the Bodhi tree in Bodh Gaya. It was under this tree that he achieved enlightenment, a profound state of awakening that allowed him to understand the true nature of existence.

The Buddha's teaching on impermanence (anicca) emphasizes that all phenomena are transient and subject to change. By understanding and accepting this impermanence, individuals can reduce their attachment to fleeting experiences and thus alleviate their suffering. The practice of mindfulness and meditation helps individuals become more aware of the present moment, allowing them to embrace life's transitory nature with equanimity.

Following his enlightenment, the Buddha devoted the remainder of his life to teaching others about the path to liberation. His teachings spread throughout Asia and eventually across the globe, influencing countless individuals and shaping spiritual practices. The Buddha's emphasis on impermanence and non-attachment provides a framework for understanding the nature of suffering and finding inner peace.

Buddhism's teachings have inspired various traditions and practices aimed at cultivating mindfulness, compassion, and wisdom. The acceptance of impermanence encourages individuals to live fully in the present moment, free from the fear of loss and change.

The life and teachings of Siddhartha Gautama, the Buddha, offer a powerful reminder of the importance of accepting the transient nature of existence. His insights into impermanence and suffering provide a pathway to inner peace and fulfillment. By embracing the principles of non-attachment and mindfulness, individuals can navigate life's changes with greater ease and find a deeper sense of contentment.

The Buddha's legacy continues to resonate with people

worldwide, demonstrating that understanding and accepting impermanence is key to achieving a more peaceful and meaningful life.

Everything in life is transient. Accepting the impermanence of all things frees you from the fear of loss and the pain of attachment. Peace comes from embracing change, not resisting it.

Whether it's a new job, a move to a new city, or the loss of a loved one, change can be scary and unsettling. But what if I told you that there is a way to not only navigate change but to actually find peace in it? The way is to accept impermanence. Peace comes from embracing change, not resisting it.

Impermanence is the understanding that everything in life is transient. Nothing lasts forever, and everything is constantly changing. This includes our relationships, our possessions, our bodies, and even our thoughts and emotions.Accepting impermanence is crucial for finding inner peace because it allows us to:

- Let go of attachment: When we accept that everything is transient, we're no longer attached to specific outcomes or possessions.

- Reduce fear: By embracing change, we reduce our fear of loss and uncertainty.

- Cultivate gratitude: Impermanence reminds us to appreciate what we have in the present moment.

- Find peace in uncertainty: By accepting that everything is constantly changing, we can find peace in the midst of uncertainty.

To accept impermanence;

- Practice mindfulness meditation to cultivate a greater awareness of the present moment.

- Reflect on your attachments and let go of those that no longer serve you.

- View change as an opportunity for growth and new experiences.

- Take time each day to reflect on what you're grateful for.

- View challenges as opportunities for growth and learning.

By accepting impermanence, we enjoy greater peace and calm, Improved relationships and Increased resilience.

Accepting impermanence is a powerful practice that can lead to a more peaceful and fulfilling life. By embracing change and letting go of attachment, we can find peace in the midst of uncertainty. Remember, impermanence is a natural part of life.

Law 20

SPEAK TRUTHFULLY, BUT KINDLY

"Kind words can be short and easy to speak, but their echoes are truly endless." - Mother Teresa

One of the most iconic events of Gandhi's leadership was the Salt March of 1930. At the time, the British government had a monopoly on salt production, imposing high taxes that burdened the Indian population. Gandhi saw this as an injustice and decided to lead a nonviolent protest against the British monopoly.

Beginning in March 1930, Gandhi, accompanied by a small group of followers, embarked on a 240-mile journey from Sabarmati Ashram to the Arabian Sea. Over 24 days, the march drew thousands of supporters, who joined in the protest by collecting salt from the sea, defying British laws. This act of civil disobedience was not only a bold political statement but also a vivid demonstration of Gandhi's philosophy in action.

The Salt March garnered international attention, highlighting the Indian independence movement and the oppressive nature of British rule. It showcased the effectiveness of nonviolent resistance and the power of speaking truthfully about injustice while maintaining a compassionate demeanor. Gandhi's approach to communication was grounded in his principle of satya (truth) and ahimsa (nonviolence). Whether addressing British authorities, Indian citizens, or international audiences, Gandhi consistently conveyed his messages with respect and empathy. He sought to build bridges of understanding rather than creating divisions.

Gandhi's principles of truth and compassion have left a lasting legacy, influencing movements for justice and human rights worldwide. His philosophy of nonviolent resistance inspired leaders such as Martin Luther King Jr. and Nelson Mandela, who adopted Gandhi's principles to their own struggles for civil rights and freedom. Gandhi's legacy serves as a powerful reminder of the impact that truthful and compassionate communication can have in the pursuit of justice. His life exemplifies how integrity, when paired with empathy, can lead to meaningful and lasting change. By advocating for nonviolence and understanding, Gandhi showed that it is possible to address deep-seated injustices while fostering a spirit of reconciliation and peace.

Mahatma Gandhi's approach to justice, rooted in the principles of Satyagraha, illustrates the profound power of speaking truthfully and compassionately. His leadership during the Salt March and his consistent emphasis on nonviolent resistance highlight how these principles can drive significant social change. Gandhi's life and teachings continue to inspire individuals and movements around the world, affirming that true progress comes from a commitment to truth and empathy in the face of adversity.

Honesty is crucial, but so is compassion. Speak your truth, but do so in a way that does not harm others. The balance of truth and kindness maintains peace in your relationships. Effective communication is the foundation of any healthy relationship, be it personal or professional. However, finding the right balance between honesty and kindness can be a daunting task. As Epictetus so wisely wrote, "Speak truthfully, but kindly. Honesty is crucial, but so is compassion. Speak your truth, but do so in a way that does not harm others."

Speaking truthfully yet kindly is essential for maintaining peace in our relationships because;

- Honesty fosters trust, while kindness shows empathy and understanding.

- Truthful words can be hurtful if not delivered with compassion.

- Kindness creates a safe space for open and honest dialogue.

- Truthful yet kind communication can diffuse tension and resolve conflicts.

To be able to speak kind words to others, choose your words wisely and consider the impact of your words on others. Be empathetic, put yourself in others' shoes and try to understand their perspective. Express your thoughts and feelings without blaming or attacking others. Hear others out and respond thoughtfully. Speak with a kind and compassionate tone. While practicing truthful yet kind communication can be challenging, there may be obstacles that get in the way and they include fear of conflict, difficulty expressing emotions and struggling to find the right words. Speaking truthfully yet kindly is a powerful practice that can lead to more peaceful and harmonious relationships. By finding the balance between honesty and compassion, we can build trust, avoid hurt, and encourage open communication. Remember, truthful yet kind communication is a skill that takes practice, so be patient and kind to yourself as you work to develop it.

Law 21

AVOID GOSSIP AND IDLE TALK

"The tongue is a small thing, but what enormous damage it can do." - Epictetus

A braham Lincoln, the 16th President of the United States, led the nation through its most turbulent period: the Civil War. His presidency was marked by immense challenges, but his ability to stay focused on critical issues while avoiding the distractions of gossip and idle talk was a cornerstone of his leadership.

Lincoln's tenure was fraught with crisis, from secession and civil war to political infighting and social upheaval. During such a tumultuous time, Lincoln's clarity of purpose and unwavering commitment to the nation's unity were essential. He understood that the distractions of gossip and petty conflicts could undermine his administration's effectiveness. Instead of allowing such distractions to dominate, Lincoln focused on the pressing issues of the time—preserving the Union and ending slavery.

One of the most critical moments of Lincoln's presidency was the crafting and issuance of the Emancipation Proclamation. This landmark decision faced significant opposition from various quarters, including members of his own cabinet, as well as critics in Congress and the general public. Some saw it as a radical move that could jeopardize the Union's war effort or inflame sectional tensions further.

Despite this opposition, Lincoln remained steadfast in his commitment to abolishing slavery. Rather than engaging in gossip or allowing dissenting voices to derail his efforts, he concentrated on the principles of justice and equality that guided his decision. His ability to stay focused on the broader goals of his presidency, even in the face of criticism and political maneuvering, was a testament to his leadership.

Lincoln's legacy is a powerful reminder of the importance of maintaining focus on meaningful goals while avoiding the pitfalls of gossip and idle talk. His leadership style demonstrated that a commitment to purpose-driven actions and respectful collaboration could lead to profound and lasting change.

By remaining focused on the critical issues of his time and fostering an environment of unity and respect, Lincoln was able to guide the nation through its darkest period. His ability to rise above personal rivalries and distractions set a standard for effective leadership that continues to be admired and studied. Abraham Lincoln's presidency exemplifies how focusing on critical issues and avoiding distractions like gossip and personal rivalries can lead to effective and transformative leadership. His ability to bring together a diverse group of advisors, remain committed to justice, and navigate through immense challenges illustrates the power of purpose-driven action. Lincoln's leadership serves as a timeless example of how clarity, respect, and unity can overcome even the most formidable obstacles, ensuring peace and progress in times of crisis.

Gossip breeds mistrust and discord. Speak only when your words are necessary and beneficial. In silence and thoughtful speech, peace is preserved. It's easy to get caught up in gossip and idle talk. Whether it's chatting with coworkers, scrolling through social media, or catching up with friends, our words can have a significant impact on ourselves and those around us. As Epictetus so wisely wrote, "Avoid gossip and idle talk. Gossip breeds mistrust and discord. Speak only when your words are necessary and beneficial. In silence and thoughtful speech, peace is preserved."

Mindful speech is crucial for maintaining peace in our lives and relationships because it:

- Thoughtful speech fosters trust, while gossip and idle talk can erode it.

- Mindful speech allows us to connect with others on a deeper level.

- Avoiding gossip and idle talk can prevent misunderstandings and conflicts.

- Mindful speech encourages us to think before speaking, leading to greater self-awareness.

To practice mindful speaking, pause before speaking; take a moment to reflect on your words before sharing them; ask yourself questions; consider whether your words are necessary, beneficial, and kind. Listen actively; pay attention to others and respond thoughtfully. Limit your engagement in gossip and idle talk and treat yourself with kindness when you slip up.

Law 22

BE CONTENT WITH SIMPLICITY

"Simplicity is the ultimate sophistication." - *Leonardo da Vinci*

Henry David Thoreau, an American essayist, poet, and philosopher, is best known for his book "Walden," which chronicles his experiment in simple living. In 1845, Thoreau chose to live alone in a small cabin near Walden Pond in Massachusetts, seeking to immerse himself in nature and reflect on the essence of life. His decision was driven by a desire to escape the complexities and materialism of society.

During his time at Walden, Thoreau embraced simplicity, focusing on essential needs and the beauty of nature. He famously wrote, "Simplify, simplify," advocating for a life free from the distractions of excess. Thoreau cultivated his own food, engaged in deep contemplation, and observed the natural world around him. This experience allowed him to connect with his inner self and understand the value of living with intention.

Thoreau's reflections on simplicity extended beyond his personal experience. He critiqued the industrial society of his time, arguing that the pursuit of wealth and possessions often led to discontent and distraction. His writing encourages readers to reevaluate their priorities and find peace in a life of moderation.

Thoreau's commitment to simplicity continues to resonate today as a powerful reminder that true contentment can be found in embracing the beauty of the present moment and letting go of the need for more

Luxury and excess often lead to envy and strife. Embrace simplicity in your lifestyle, finding joy in what you have rather than in the pursuit of more. Contentment is the bedrock of peace.
We're constantly bombarded with messages telling us that we need the latest gadget, the trendiest clothes, and the most luxurious possessions to be happy. Luxury and excess often lead to envy and strife. Embrace simplicity in your lifestyle, finding joy in what you have rather than in the pursuit of more. Contentment is the bedrock of peace.

Excess and luxury may seem appealing, but they can lead to envy and comparison, financial stress and debt, clutter and disorganization, dissatisfaction and discontent and strife and conflict. Embracing simplicity, on the other hand, can bring, Contentment and peace, financial freedom and security, clarity and focus, gratitude and appreciation and connection and community.

To practice simplicity, declutter your space, get rid of unnecessary possessions and create a peaceful environment. Simplify your wardrobe, focus on quality over quantity and adopt a capsule wardrobe. Cook simple meals, prepare nourishing, whole-food meals that bring you joy.

Practice mindfulness, focus on the present moment and let go of distractions. Cultivate gratitude, reflect on the things you're thankful for each day.

Embracing simplicity is a powerful practice that can lead to greater peace, contentment, and fulfillment. By letting go of excess and focusing on what truly matters, we can find joy in what we have rather than constantly pursuing more. Remember, simplicity is a journey, not a destination. Be patient, kind, and compassionate with yourself as you work to cultivate contentment in a world of excess.

Law 23

MASTER THE ART OF LETTING GO

"The art of letting go is the art of living." - Unknown

Nelson Mandela, the first black president of South Africa and a prominent anti-apartheid revolutionary, exemplified the art of letting go. Born in 1918, Mandela spent 27 years in prison for his resistance to the apartheid regime. Despite enduring harsh conditions and significant personal loss, he emerged with a profound understanding of forgiveness and reconciliation.

While imprisoned, Mandela reflected on the importance of letting go of resentment and anger. He recognized that holding onto such emotions would only perpetuate the cycle of violence and division in his country. Upon his release in 1990, Mandela advocated for a peaceful transition from apartheid to a democratic South Africa, prioritizing healing over vengeance.

In 1994, Mandela was elected president and established the Truth and Reconciliation Commission, aimed at addressing the atrocities of apartheid through dialogue and understanding rather than punishment. His willingness to let go of past grievances and embrace a vision of unity helped heal a fractured nation. He famously stated, "Resentment is like drinking poison and then hoping it will kill your enemies," illustrating his commitment to the power of letting go.

Mandela's legacy teaches us that mastering the art of letting go is essential for personal and societal peace. His journey from prisoner to president serves as a reminder that forgiveness and understanding can pave the way for healing and progress, even in the most challenging circumstances.

Peace requires the ability to let go—of possessions, relationships, and even life itself when the time comes. The more you practice detachment, the more unshakable your peace becomes. Do you often find yourself holding onto things, emotions, or relationships that no longer serve you? Do you struggle with the idea of letting go, fearing that it will lead to loss or emptiness? You're not alone. Many of us have been conditioned to believe that holding on is a sign of strength, when in fact, it's often a sign of fear.

Letting go is a powerful practice that can lead to inner peace, emotional liberation, and spiritual renewal. In this blog, we'll explore the transformative power of letting go and provide practical tips on how to release the things that no longer serve you.

Letting go can be challenging because it requires us to confront our fears, insecurities, and attachment to specific outcomes. We may fear that letting go will lead to:

- Loss of control: We may feel that holding on gives us a sense of control over our lives and circumstances.

- Emotional pain: Letting go can lead to feelings of sadness, grief, and loss.

- Uncertainty: We may fear the unknown and what will happen if we let go.

- Regret: We may worry that we'll regret our decision to let go.

However, holding onto these things can lead to emotional stagnation which can prevent us from moving forward and growing, mental exhaustion that may lead to fatigue and burnout, physical tension, and spiritual disconnection from our true selves and the present moment.

Law 24

FOSTER A GRATEFUL HEART

"Gratitude unlocks the fullness of life. It turns what we have into enough, and more." - Melody Beattie

Oprah Winfrey, one of the most influential media personalities in the world, embodies the principle of fostering a grateful heart. Born into poverty in rural Mississippi, Winfrey faced numerous challenges throughout her childhood, including abuse and instability. However, she cultivated a profound sense of gratitude that would ultimately shape her life and career.

From a young age, Winfrey recognized the importance of gratitude in overcoming adversity. She often reflected on the support she received from mentors and the small joys in her life, such as her grandmother's encouragement and the power of education. This grateful perspective propelled her to excel academically, earning a scholarship to Tennessee State University.

Winfrey's career in media began when she became the first black female news anchor at Nashville's WLAC-TV. Her authentic storytelling and empathetic approach resonated with audiences, leading to the launch of "The Oprah Winfrey Show" in 1986. Throughout her career, she emphasized the importance of gratitude, often sharing her reflections on how it transforms one's outlook on life.

In 2006, Winfrey launched the "Oprah's Big Give" initiative, encouraging acts of kindness and generosity. She also founded the Oprah Winfrey Foundation, which focuses on education and empowerment. Winfrey's life and career demonstrate that fostering a grateful heart not only brings personal fulfillment but also inspires others and creates positive change.

Imagine living in a state of perpetual discontent, where every day feels like a struggle and every experience is tinged with disappointment. This is the reality for many of us, stuck in a cycle of negativity and dissatisfaction. Gratitude is a powerful antidote to discontent. Regularly count your blessings and express thanks for what you have. A grateful heart is a peaceful heart.

By focusing on what we already have, rather than what's lacking, we can begin to shift our perspective and transform our lives. Gratitude has a profound impact on our well-being, influencing everything from our relationships to our physical health. When we practice gratitude, our brains release dopamine, a neurotransmitter associated with pleasure and reward.

Practicing gratitude has a range of benefits, which includes, improved relationships, increased self-esteem, better sleep quality and improved physical health. However gratitude is more than just a feeling, it's a practice. And like any practice, it takes effort and dedication to cultivate.

Gratitude has the power to transform our lives, to turn what we have into enough, and to reveal the fullness of life. To practice gratitude, you will need to keep a gratitude journal and write down three things you are thankful for each day. Share your gratitude with others, whether it's a kind word or a small gift, practice mindfulness, taking time to appreciate the present moment and reframe negative thoughts. Try to find the silver lining in every situation.

Gratitude is especially important during difficult times. When we're faced with challenges, it's easy to get caught up in negative thoughts and feelings of discontent. But by focusing on what we're grateful for, we can begin to shift our perspective and find peace in the midst of turmoil. By incorporating gratitude into our daily practice, we can begin to shift our perspective and find joy in the present moment.

Law 25

EMBRACE SOLITUDE

"Solitude is the soil in which the seeds of wisdom are sown." - Unknown

G race was tired of the city life, the honking cars, factory noise and everything in between. She was not cut out for that kind of life. She always felt drained at the end of the day, having spent the day running errands and working. She felt overwhelmed by the constant chatter, the endless distractions, and the pressure to conform.

She was an introvert whose job forced to be outgoing. She liked to be in a quiet and serene environment. Grace realized that she had been reacting to the world around her, rather than responding from a place of inner peace. She began to embrace solitude, seeking out quiet moments to reflect, to meditate, and to connect with her own heart.

As Grace spent more time in solitude, she found that her mind grew clearer, her heart grew wiser, and her spirit grew stronger. She learned to listen to her own inner voice, to trust her own intuition, and to find guidance from within. Solitude is the soil in which the seeds of wisdom are sown.

Solitude is often viewed as a luxury or an anomaly. We're constantly bombarded with messages telling us to stay connected, engage with others, and avoid being alone. However, this relentless push for social interaction can lead to a neglect of one of the most essential aspects of human experience: solitude.

Solitude, or the state of being alone, is a powerful catalyst for personal growth, self-discovery, and transformation. By embracing solitude, we can tap into our inner selves, explore our thoughts and emotions, and develop a deeper understanding of who we are and what we want out of life. Solitude is not loneliness but a refuge. Regularly seek time alone to recharge and reflect. In solitude, you can reconnect with your inner peace.

Solitude has numerous benefits that can positively impact various aspects of our lives. Some of these benefits include:

- Improved mental clarity and focus: Solitude allows us to quiet the mind, reduce distractions, and concentrate on our thoughts and goals.

- Increased self-awareness: By spending time alone, we can develop a better understanding of our values, beliefs, and motivations.

- Enhanced creativity: Solitude can foster creativity, as it allows us to explore new ideas, reflect on our experiences, and think outside the box.

- Better decision-making: With solitude, we can weigh our options, consider different perspectives, and make more informed decisions.

- Reduced stress and anxiety: Solitude provides an opportunity to relax, unwind, and recharge, leading to a reduction in stress and anxiety.

By embracing solitude, you will discover a powerful secret that true wisdom, creativity, and innovation arise from the depths of our own inner world. Solitude is the foundation of a life of wisdom, peace, and purpose.

Research has shown that solitude has a profound impact on our brain function, behavior, and overall well-being. When we're alone, our brains enter a state of default mode, which allows us to reflect on our experiences and memories, explore our thoughts and emotions, develop a sense of self and identity, improve our problem-solving skills and enhance our creativity and imagination

Incorporating solitude into our daily lives can be challenging, but there are several strategies that can help and they include;

- Scheduling alone time: Set aside time each day or week for solitude, whether it's reading, meditating, or simply sitting in silence.

- Finding a quiet space: Identify a quiet, comfortable space where you can retreat from the world and focus on yourself.

- Practicing mindfulness: Use mindfulness techniques, such as deep breathing or meditation, to quiet the mind and focus on the present moment.

- Engaging in solo activities: Participate in activities that bring you joy and fulfillment, such as writing, painting, or hiking.

- Learning to say no: Establish boundaries and prioritize self-care by learning to say no to social invitations that drain your energy.

Solitude is a powerful way to cultivate personal growth, self-awareness, and transformation. By incorporating alone time into our daily lives, we can tap into our inner selves, explore our thoughts and emotions, and develop a deeper understanding of who we are and what we want out of life. Remember, solitude is not a luxury or an anomaly, but a necessity for living a happy, healthy, and fulfilling life.

Law 26

LIVE IN ACCORDANCE WITH YOUR VALUES

"The best way to find yourself is to lose yourself in the service of others." - Mahatma Gandhi

In ancient Athens, Socrates was known not just for his philosophy, but for his steadfast commitment to living by his principles. He was relentless in his pursuit of truth, even when it put him at odds with the powerful elites of the city.

In 399 BCE, Socrates was brought to trial on charges of corrupting the youth and impiety, essentially for questioning the status quo. The Athenians offered him a way out: if he renounced his beliefs, he would be spared execution. Many of his friends, including Plato, urged him to do so, believing that it was better to live even if it meant compromising his values.

But Socrates refused. He famously stated that "the unexamined life is not worth living." He knew that to compromise his values for the sake of survival would be to betray everything he stood for. His decision to drink the hemlock, even though it led to his death, was a powerful statement: Socrates would rather die with integrity than live a life devoid of the truth he held so dear.

Socrates's life exemplifies how living in alignment with one's values brings peace, even in the face of extreme adversity. His decision to stand by his beliefs, knowing it would cost him his life, reveals that peace is not about avoiding conflict or discomfort. Rather, it is about knowing and embracing your core values, letting them guide your decisions. When your actions reflect your deepest truths, inner peace follows, regardless of external circumstances.

The pursuit of peace and fulfillment is a universal human aspiration. Yet, many of us struggle to find lasting satisfaction in our lives. We often attribute this to external circumstances, but the truth lies within. The key to unlocking peace and fulfillment is to live in accordance with our deepest values. Peace is the byproduct of a life lived in alignment with your deepest values. Know what matters to you and let those values guide your decisions and actions.

Your values are the foundation upon which you build your life. They are the principles that guide your decisions, actions, and relationships. When you live in alignment with your values, you experience a sense of purpose, direction, and fulfillment. Conversely, when you compromise on your values, you may feel lost, unfulfilled, and disconnected from your true self.

To live in accordance with your values, you must first identify what they are. Take time to reflect on the following questions:

- What matters most to me in life?

- What do I stand for?

- What do I believe in?

- What kind of person do I want to be?

Your values may include qualities such as authenticity, empathy, courage, creativity, family or freedom. Once you have identified your core values, it is essential to integrate them into your daily life. Making value-based decisions can help you integrate your values into your life. When faced with a decision, ask yourself which option aligns with your values. You should also prioritize your time, spend your time on activities that align with your values. Set boundaries, it is important to learn to say no to things that do not align with your values. Surround yourself with like-minded people, spending time with people who share your values is key. And lastly, practice self-reflection, regularly reflect on your actions and decisions to ensure they align with your values.

When you live in accordance with your values, you experience a profound sense of peace and fulfillment. This is because your actions and decisions are guided by a deep sense of purpose and direction. You feel more connected to your true self and more confident in your choices.

By identifying your core values and integrating them into your daily life, you can experience a sense of purpose, direction, and satisfaction that eludes many people. Remember, your values are the foundation of your life. Take the time to discover them, and make them the guiding force behind your decisions and actions.

Law 27

DO NOT SEEK EXTERNAL VALIDATION

"You alone are enough. You have nothing to prove to anyone." - Maya Angelou

I n the early 1600s, Galileo Galilei, an Italian astronomer, made groundbreaking discoveries that shook the foundations of established science and the authority of the Church. Through his telescope, Galileo observed moons orbiting Jupiter and the phases of Venus, offering proof that not everything in the heavens revolved around the Earth. His observations supported the heliocentric theory proposed by Copernicus, which placed the Sun, not the Earth, at the center of the universe.

Despite the evidence, Galileo faced fierce opposition from the Church and many scholars who clung to the geocentric view. His ideas were declared heretical, and he was eventually summoned to face the Inquisition. Galileo had a choice: recant his discoveries to gain the approval of the Church and avoid severe punishment, or stand by the truth he had uncovered, risking his reputation and safety.

Galileo chose the latter. Although he was forced to publicly recant his heliocentric views to avoid execution, he never truly abandoned them. Legend has it that, after his recantation, he whispered, "And yet it moves," referring to the Earth. Galileo's refusal to seek external validation cost him his freedom—he spent the rest of his life under house arrest but he remained at peace, knowing he had stayed true to his pursuit of truth.

Had he craved approval from others, he might have easily abandoned his discoveries to fit into the societal mold. But by seeking validation from within; grounded in his understanding of scientific truth and commitment to knowledge, he found peace, even in adversity. Galileo's legacy stands as a reminder that relying on others for approval compromises both integrity and inner peace. True fulfillment comes from within, from knowing your worth and staying committed to your principles.

Seeking approval and validation from others to feel good about ourselves is very common in our world today. But the truth is, this approach can be detrimental to our mental and emotional well-being. Relying on external validation can lead to a never-ending cycle of seeking approval, which can be exhausting and unfulfilling. It's like constantly trying to prove ourselves to others, without ever feeling truly secure or confident.

Relying on others for validation disrupts your peace. Seek

approval from within, grounded in your understanding of your worth and your commitment to your principles. The problem is, when we rely on others for validation, we're giving away our power. We're saying, "I need you to make me feel good about myself." But what happens when that person is gone, or they're not available, or they're not interested? We're left feeling lost and insecure.

So, what's the alternative? Self-validation. It's about learning to love and accept ourselves, flaws and all. It's about recognizing our strengths and accomplishments, and celebrating them. It's about being kind to ourselves, and treating ourselves with compassion and understanding.

By focusing on self-validation, we can start to feel more confident, more self-assured, and more at peace. We'll realize that we don't need anyone else's approval to be worthy, because we're already enough.

By developing self-awareness, self-acceptance, and self-compassion, you can learn to validate yourself and find peace in your own skin. Breaking free from the need for external validation takes courage, but it's a journey worth taking. By finding validation within, you can cultivate a deeper sense of self-worth, self-trust, and peace. Remember, your worth is not defined by others; it's defined by your commitment to your principles and your unwavering belief in yourself.

Law 28

AVOID ENVY

"Envy is the ulcer of the soul." - Socrates

Sophia struggled with envy, her mother had two children. Both were girls, Sophia was the eldest. She envied the care her sister got from their mother and wished to take her sister's place. She also behaved as if she was in a competition with her sister, how she dressed, talked and even her job were carefully chosen to outshine her sister.

Her sister was oblivious to this, she lived life as she wanted, pursued her dream job and married her dream man. Sophia couldn't help but compare herself to others, and felt resentful of their successes. It was as if she was not progressing, the success she achieved always looked small compared to what her sister and others achieved.

Frustrated and angry, Sophia reached out to Matt, her best friend. She told him how she thinks she was stagnant and how her sister was progressing. Matt suspected that Sophie was filled with envy and resentment, he reminded her of the importance of contentment and why she should avoid envy.

He told her that an envious person always sees the progress of others but never his own. He advised her to let go of envy and focus on herself. Sophia realized that her envy was a result of her own reactions and perceptions. She began to focus on her own path and celebrate the successes of others without comparison.

As Sophia avoided envy, she found a sense of peace and contentment that she had never known before. She was no longer consumed by negative emotions, and was able to cultivate meaningful relationships with others.
She was also able to live a life of true harmony and inner peace.

Envy is a feeling of discontent, resentment, and jealousy towards someone else's success, achievements, or possessions. It's a negative emotion that arises when we perceive someone else as having something we desire, but feel we cannot attain.

Envy is corrosive to peace. Focus on your own path and celebrate the successes of others without comparison. By avoiding envy, you maintain harmony. Envy can have negative consequences, such as damaged relationships, mental health issues, and missed opportunities.

Envy can also be manifested in various ways, such as resentment, jealousy, inadequacy and longing. Feeling bitter or indignant towards someone who has achieved something we want, a feeling of being threatened or insecure about someone else's success or possessions, intensely desiring something someone else has, often accompanied by a sense of entitlement and insufficiency compared to someone else is a sign of envy.

When we allow envy to take hold, it eats away at our inner harmony, causing us to feel anxious, insecure, and dissatisfied with our own lives. To avoid the poison of envy and cultivate harmony and peace instead the first step is to focus on your own path. Instead of comparing yourself to others, concentrate on your own goals, values, and aspirations. Celebrate your own successes, no matter how small they may seem. Remember, everyone's journey is unique, and comparisons only lead to feelings of inadequacy.

When you see someone else's success, try to practice empathy and understanding. Put yourself in their shoes and acknowledge the hard work and dedication that led to their achievement. Remember that everyone faces challenges and setbacks, and success is often the result of perseverance and resilience.

Gratitude is a powerful antidote to envy. When you focus on what you already have, rather than what you lack, you begin to see the world in a different light. Keep a gratitude journal, write down three things you're thankful for each day, or share your gratitude with a friend or loved one.

Finally, celebrate others' successes without comparison. Be genuinely happy for your friends, colleagues, and acquaintances when they achieve their goals. Remember that their success doesn't diminish your own worth or value.

Law 29

CULTIVATE PATIENCE

"Patience is bitter but the fruit is sweet" - Aristotle.

L eo loved to cook; he would spend his time helping his mother in the kitchen as a kid. His father noticed his love for cooking and enrolled him for a cooking class when he clocked 16. Leo was very excited and couldn't wait to become a professional.

His excitement died after the first two weeks; cooking was not as simple as he thought. He had to retake his practicals several times before he could master them. He struggled with impatience. He wanted to achieve enlightenment quickly and easily, but found himself frustrated with the slow pace of his progress.

His Tutor observed Leo's impatience and frustration, then called him into his office where he counseled him on the importance of patience. Leo realized that his impatience was a result of his own reactions and expectations. He began to focus on the present moment and let go of his attachment to specific outcomes.

As Leo cultivated patience, he found a sense of peace and clarity that he had never known before. He was no longer controlled by his emotions and was able to approach challenges with a calm and gentle spirit.

The impediment to action advances action. What stands in the way becomes the way. Leo's patience had become the way, allowing him to move forward with wisdom and grace. Cultivating patience takes practice, but it's worth it. To build peace practice mindfulness; take a few minutes each day to focus on your breath, your body, and your surroundings.

Patience is the ability to endure difficult circumstances with calmness and composure. It's the capacity to wait, to persevere, and to trust that things will work out in the end. Patience is not about being passive or apathetic; it's about being present and mindful in the face of challenges.

Epictetus so wisely said, "Patience is the best remedy for every trouble." Peace often requires patience, whether in dealing with others or in waiting for your efforts to bear fruit. Cultivate patience as a virtue, and peace will naturally follow.

In a world that values speed and efficiency, patience can seem like a luxury we can't afford. But the truth is, patience is essential for achieving peace. When we're patient, we're able to:

- Approach challenges with clarity and calmness

- Build stronger, more meaningful relationships

- Make better decisions, unclouded by emotions

- Trust in the natural unfolding of life

Set realistic expectations, understand that things take time, and that setbacks are a natural part of the journey. You should also take breaks, give yourself permission to rest and recharge. And lastly, practice gratitude, focus on the good things in your life, no matter how small they may seem.

When we cultivate patience, we open ourselves up to a range of benefits which includes reduced stress and anxiety, improved relationships, increased self-awareness and greater sense of calm and clarity

Patience is a virtue that's more important than ever in our world today. By cultivating patience, we can achieve a deeper sense of peace, clarity, and calm. Remember, patience is not about waiting for things to happen; it's about trusting in the natural unfolding of life. So take a deep breath, slow down, and trust that everything will work out in the end.

Law 30

PRACTICE HUMILITY

"Humility is the foundation of all wisdom." - *Epictetus*

Geroge Washington, the first President of the United States, is often cited for his humility and reluctance to cling to power. Born in 1732, Washington was a key figure in the American Revolutionary War and played a crucial role in the founding of the United States. His leadership during the war and his subsequent presidency demonstrated a profound sense of humility and a commitment to democratic principles.

After the Revolutionary War, Washington was offered the opportunity to become a king or dictator, but he refused these offers, choosing instead to return to his private life. His decision to step down after two terms as President in 1797 set a precedent for the peaceful transfer of power in American politics.

Washington's reluctance to remain in power and his willingness to relinquish authority were significant contributions to the establishment of a democratic government. His actions exemplified the principle of humility, showing that true leadership involves prioritizing the greater good over personal ambition.

Washington's legacy of humility and dedication to democratic values continues to inspire leaders and citizens alike. His example underscores that exercising humility is essential for building trust, fostering collaboration, and ensuring the stability and integrity of institutions.

It is easy to get caught up in the idea that we need to have all the answers. We are in a generation where we are constantly bombarded with information and advice, and we are often encouraged to project an image of confidence and expertise. But the truth is, none of us have all the answers. And that's okay.In fact, recognizing our limitations and practicing humility can be a powerful path to peace. Recognize that you do not know everything, and you do not need to. Humility opens you to learning and growth, fostering a deep and abiding peace.

Humility is the quality of being modest and unassuming. It's the recognition that we do not have all the answers, and that we can always learn and grow. Humility is not about being weak or lacking confidence; it's about being honest and authentic. Humility can seem like a weakness, especially in a world that often values confidence and expertise, but the truth is, humility is a strength. When we practice humility, we open ourselves up to learning and growth, build stronger, more meaningful relationships, develop a greater sense of empathy and compassion and cultivate a deeper sense of inner peace.

Practicing humility takes effort and intention, but it's worth it. Recognize your limitations and acknowledge that you don't have all the answers. Try to listen more than you speak, pay attention to others and learn from their experiences. Ask questions and seek guidance and wisdom from others. You should learn to change your mind, don't be afraid to admit when you're wrong. When we practice humility, we experience greater sense of peace and calm, deeper, more meaningful relationships and increased empathy and compassion. Humility is strength. By recognizing our limitations and practicing humility, we can cultivate a deeper sense of inner peace and open ourselves up to learning and growth.

Law 31

R E S P O N D , D O N O T
R E A C T

"The universe is changing; our life is what our thoughts make it." - Marcus Aurelius

In 1863, during the American Civil War, General Ulysses S. Grant faced significant pressure as he led the Union Army. After a series of costly battles, public sentiment turned against him, and he was criticized heavily in the press. Instead of reacting impulsively or defensively, Grant took a deliberate approach. He focused on his strategy rather than the opinions of others, reminding himself that his duty was to the men under his command and the mission at hand. This stoic mindset allowed him to maintain his resolve and ultimately achieve victory at Vicksburg. By responding thoughtfully rather than reacting emotionally, Grant preserved not only his peace of mind but also the morale of his troops, leading to a crucial turning point in the war.

Have you ever found yourself in a situation where you have reacted impulsively, only to regret your words or actions later? Maybe you have lashed out at a loved one, sent an angry email, or spoken out of turn in a meeting. We have all been there.

In moments of conflict, pause and choose your response rather than reacting instinctively. This deliberation will often diffuse tension and maintain peace. Reacting and responding may look similar but they are different. Reacting is instinctive; it's a knee-jerk response to a situation, often driven by emotions like fear, anger, or frustration. Reacting can lead to hurtful words, damaged relationships, and regret.

Responding, on the other hand, is thoughtful; it's a considered reaction that takes into account the situation, the other person's perspective, and our own values and goals. Responding allows us to choose our words and actions wisely, leading to greater understanding and peace.

Thoughtful responses can become a source of strength and wisdom, allowing her to navigate life's challenges with greater ease and peace. A few benefit of responding includes;

- Diffuses tension: A pause can calm the emotions and create space for rational thinking.

- Encourages empathy: By considering the other person's perspective, we can respond with compassion and understanding.

- Fosters clarity: A pause allows us to gather our thoughts and respond with clarity and purpose.

- Builds trust: When we respond thoughtfully, we build trust with others and demonstrate our commitment to understanding.

Incorporating the power of pausing into your daily life is simpler than you think, firstly take a deep breath: When you feel yourself reacting, take a deep breath and pause. Step away, Sometimes, taking a break from the situation can help you clear your head and respond thoughtfully. You should also ask questions, seek clarification and understanding before responding. And practice mindfulness, you can build mindfulness through meditation or other practices to increase your self-awareness and ability to pause. Do not value quick reactions and instant gratification, the power of pause can be a game-changer. By choosing to respond instead of react, we can create space for understanding, empathy, and peace. Remember, the next time you find yourself in a moment of conflict to take a deep breath, pause, and choose your response wisely. The results may just transform your life.

Law 32

SEEK INNER WISDOM

"Wisdom is the supreme part of happiness." - *Sophocles*

Socrates, the revered ancient Greek philosopher, is renowned for his relentless pursuit of wisdom and his commitment to living a life of philosophical inquiry. One of the most poignant stories reflecting his dedication to wisdom occurs in the context of his trial and eventual execution, specifically during a conversation with Criton, a wealthy Athenian friend.

In 399 BCE, Socrates was sentenced to death by the Athenian court on charges of impiety and corrupting the youth of Athens. This sentence came after a trial where Socrates, known for his dialectical method and challenge to established norms, had been found guilty. The punishment was to be carried out by consuming a drink containing poison hemlock.

Facing this grim reality, Socrates remained composed and unperturbed. He was not swayed by fear or despair but approached his final days with the same philosophical rigor he had applied throughout his life. Criton, a wealthy and influential friend of Socrates, visited him in prison, deeply distressed by the philosopher's impending execution. Criton urged Socrates to escape from prison and avoid the death sentence, offering to provide the means for a safe escape. He argued that Socrates' death would be a loss not only to himself but to the many who would benefit from his wisdom and teachings.

Socrates, however, responded with a calm and reasoned perspective. He urged Criton to think beyond the immediate pressures and concerns of public opinion or material loss. Socrates emphasized that the pursuit of wisdom and the adherence to principles of justice were far more important than the opinions of the majority or the preservation of his own life.

Socrates told Criton that true wisdom is not found in wealth, comfort, or public approval, but in the steadfast commitment to living a life guided by inner principles and ethical integrity. He argued that one should not make decisions based solely on popular opinion but should instead focus on what is just and right according to reason and moral understanding.

Socrates' unwavering commitment to his philosophical beliefs and his calm acceptance of his fate illustrate his deep understanding of the importance of inner wisdom. He viewed his impending death not as an end but as an opportunity to demonstrate his philosophical ideals. For Socrates, maintaining integrity and adhering to one's principles was more significant than life itself.

Socrates' life and final moments exemplify how the pursuit of wisdom and the adherence to one's principles can lead to profound inner peace, regardless of external circumstances. His story teaches that true fulfillment and peace are achieved not through material wealth or societal approval but through a life lived with integrity and thoughtful reflection.

Inner wisdom is the culmination of our experiences, knowledge, and intuition. It's the quiet voice within us that knows what's best, even when the world around us is loud and uncertain. Inner wisdom is developed through learning, you can acquire knowledge and understanding through study and exploration.

Experience and challenges can help you gain insight and perspective, reflection or taking time to think, meditate, and connect with your inner self can help you to develop inner wisdom.

In a world that's increasingly external-focused, inner wisdom is more crucial than ever. By cultivating inner wisdom, we develop clarity, purpose, make better decisions, build resilience and confidence and experience true peace and contentment. To build your inner wisdom, practice mindfulness and meditation, take time for self-reflection and journaling, seek out new experiences and learning opportunities and listen to your intuition and trust your instincts.

True peace is guided by wisdom. Cultivate your inner wisdom through learning, experience, and reflection. Let this wisdom guide your actions and decisions. In a world that's full of noise and distractions, it's easy to lose sight of what's truly important. But by seeking inner wisdom, we can find peace, clarity, and purpose. Remember, the greatest source of guidance and wisdom lies within you. Take the time to cultivate it, and watch your life transform in profound ways.

Law 33

HONOR YOUR COMMITMENTS

"Integrity is doing the right thing, even when no one is watching." - C.S. Lewis

In 1940, during World War II, British Prime Minister Winston Churchill delivered his famous "We shall fight on the beaches" speech to the House of Commons. Churchill had made a commitment to the British people to stand firm against Nazi Germany. Despite facing overwhelming odds and the threat of invasion, he understood the importance of honoring his commitments. His resolve inspired a nation, fostering unity and determination during a time of uncertainty. Churchill's unwavering dedication to his promises served as a beacon of hope, demonstrating that true leadership lies in honoring one's commitments, even in the face of adversity.

Want to know a secret to achieving peace and prosperity? It's simple: honor your commitments! Think about it, when you keep your promises, you build trust, strengthen relationships, and earn respect from others and yourself. We damage relationships, feel guilty and anxious, and miss out on opportunities when we are not honest. It's easy to make promises and commitments without fully thinking through the consequences. We may overcommit, forget, or simply change our minds, leaving others feeling let down and distrustful.

When we honor our commitments, we build trust and credibility with others. We develop a clear conscience and sense of integrity. Strengthen our relationships and foster deeper connections. Experience increased self-respect and confidence, and enjoy peace and inner calm. When we fail to honor our commitments, we damage relationships, erode trust, experience guilt, shame, and anxiety, miss opportunities and lose credibility, and struggle with self-doubt and low self-esteem.

Honour your words and be honest by being mindful of your commitments. Think carefully before making promises or agreements. Keep track of your commitments, you can write them down, set reminders, and stay organized. Don't be afraid to communicate openly, if you need to adjust or cancel a commitment, communicate honestly and promptly. Take responsibility; own up to your mistakes and make amends when necessary.
Practice self-reflection, regularly examine your commitments and priorities.

Integrity is often overlooked, honoring your commitments is a powerful way to stand out and build strong relationships. By keeping your promises and being true to your word, you'll experience peace, self-respect, and a clear conscience. Remember, your word is your bond, use it wisely and watch your life flourish. Peace arises from integrity. Honor your commitments and keep your promises. When your word is trusted, your relationships and self-respect flourish.

Law 34

PRACTICE DETACHMENT FROM PRAISE AND CRITICISM

"The universe is indifferent to your opinions." - Epictetus

The life of the renowned artist Vincent van Gogh provides a powerful example of practicing detachment from both praise and criticism. During his lifetime, Van Gogh produced over 2,000 artworks, yet he sold only a handful. Critics often dismissed his work, and he struggled with self-doubt. However, Van Gogh remained committed to his passion, painting for the sake of expression rather than for external validation. His letters to his brother Theo reveal a deep understanding of the importance of focusing on his inner vision rather than seeking approval. Today, Van Gogh is celebrated as one of the greatest artists in history, illustrating that true peace comes from valuing one's own judgment above the fleeting opinions of others.

When we rely on others for validation, we give away our power. We become puppets on strings, dancing to the tune of other people's opinions. Detachment is not about ignoring others or being aloof. It's about finding your own inner strength and self-worth. It's about learning to value yourself, regardless of what others think. Detach by focusing on your own goals and values. Practice mindfulness and self-awareness. Seek constructive feedback, but don't let it define your self-worth, and surround yourself with positive, supportive people

It's time to take back control of your life. It's time to find your own inner peace and self-worth. Remember, your worth isn't defined by others, it's defined by you. When we seek validation from others, we give away our power. We become dependent on their opinions, and our self-worth rises and falls with their praise and criticism. This is a fragile existence, subject to the whims of others.

Detachment is not about ignoring others or being aloof. It's about finding a sense of inner peace and self-worth that isn't dependent on external validation. By practicing detachment, you'll find freedom from the cycle of praise and criticism. You'll discover a sense of purpose and direction that comes from within. Remember, your worth isn't defined by others, it's defined by you.

Neither praise nor criticism should overly influence your peace. Stay grounded in your own self-assessment, valuing constructive feedback while remaining centered in your own judgment.

Law 35

PRIORITIZE PEACE OVER BEING RIGHT

"Peace is the only battle worth waging." - Albert Camus

During the Cuban Missile Crisis in October 1962, President John F. Kennedy faced one of the most perilous moments in American history. Tensions escalated as the United States discovered Soviet missiles in Cuba. In this high-stakes scenario, Kennedy prioritized peace over being right. He understood that a military confrontation could lead to catastrophic consequences. Instead of rushing to a decision, he opted for a careful and diplomatic approach, opting for a naval blockade and negotiations rather than a full-blown invasion. Kennedy's willingness to prioritize peace over the pressure to be decisive ultimately defused the crisis, demonstrating that sometimes the greater victory lies in maintaining peace rather than proving a point.

Winning an argument might seem like a victory, but at what cost? We have all been caught up in the heat of the moment, determined to prove a point and emerge victorious. But in the end, what do we really gain? A hollow sense of triumph, a strained relationship, and a lingering feeling of unrest. Epictetus, the ancient Greek philosopher, offers a profound insight, "Prioritize peace over being right." It's a simple yet powerful message that can transform the way we interact with others and ourselves.

Our need to be right is a toxic obsession that can consume us. It drives us to argue, to debate, and to prove a point, no matter the cost. We become so focused on winning that we lose sight of what truly matters; connection, understanding, and peace. But why do we feel this need so intensely? Often, it's tied to our ego and our sense of self-worth. We believe that being right validates our identity and proves our intelligence. But this is a flawed approach. Our worth and value come from who we are, not from being right.

Winning an argument often comes at the cost of peace. Learn to let go of the need to be right, prioritizing peace in your interactions over proving a point. Winning an argument might feel good at the moment, but it often comes at a steep price. We damage relationships, create conflict, and miss opportunities for growth and understanding. And for what? So we can say we're right?

The truth is, being right is not as important as we think. In fact, it's often a barrier to true connection and understanding. When we prioritize being right, we create conflict , tension, damage relationships and trust, miss opportunities for growth and learning and lose sight of what truly matters.

Surrendering our need to be right is not about being weak or passive. It's about being courageous, wise, and open. When we let go of the need to win, we create space for:

- Deeper connections and relationships

- Inner peace and calm

- Growth and understanding

- Freedom from the need to control

To prioritize peace over being right, listen actively and empathetically, seek understanding, not victory, ask open-ended questions, focus on the issue, not the person and be willing to yield and compromise

Prioritizing peace over being right is a journey, not a destination. It takes courage, self-awareness, and a willingness to let go. But the reward is worth it - deeper connections, inner peace, and a sense of freedom from the need to control.

Law 36

LET YOUR ACTIONS SPEAK

"Actions speak louder than words." - Epictetus

The life of Mahatma Gandhi exemplifies the principle of letting actions speak louder than words. In 1930, Gandhi initiated the Salt March, a 240-mile journey to protest British colonial laws that taxed salt. Instead of resorting to violence or heated rhetoric, he embodied the principle of nonviolent resistance. His commitment to peaceful protest galvanized millions of Indians, drawing international attention to their struggle for independence. Through this act of civil disobedience, Gandhi's actions spoke volumes, inspiring a movement that would ultimately lead to India's independence in 1947. Gandhi's legacy reminds us that our actions can be a powerful testament to our beliefs and principles.

Words are powerful, but they have their limits. We can talk about peace all day, but if our actions don't align with our words, we're just paying lip service. It's easy to get caught up in the theory of peace, but it's much harder to put it into practice. That is because peace isn't just a feeling or a state of mind, it's a choice. It's a choice to act with kindness, compassion, and understanding, even when it's hard. It's a choice to prioritize empathy over ego, and to seek common ground over conflict.

Actions have the power to inspire. When we let our conduct speak louder than our words, we create a ripple effect of peace that can spread far and wide. We inspire others to do the same, creating a wave of kindness and compassion that can change the world.

Your actions can speak through;

- Practice empathy and active listening

- Seek common ground and compromise

- Act with kindness and compassion, even when it's hard

- Prioritize understanding over being right

- Be mindful of your impact on others

In the pursuit of peace, actions are more powerful than words. Let your conduct reflect your commitment to peace, and others will be inspired by your example. Letting your actions speak louder than your words is a powerful way to pursue peace. It's not always easy, but it's always worth it. Remember, peace isn't just a feeling or a state of mind, it's a choice. And when we choose to act with kindness, compassion, and understanding, we create a world of peace that inspires others to do the same. So, let your conduct speak louder than your words. Choose peace.

Law 37

CULTIVATE INNER FORTITUDE

"Life doesn't get easier or more forgiving, we get stronger and more resilient." - Steve Maraboli

Nelson Mandela's journey from prisoner to president is a testament to cultivating inner fortitude. Imprisoned for 27 years, Mandela faced immense challenges but never wavered in his resolve. Instead of succumbing to despair, he focused on inner strength and resilience. During his time in prison, he studied, reflected, and forged connections with fellow inmates. His inner fortitude allowed him to envision a peaceful, democratic South Africa. Upon his release in 1990, he advocated for reconciliation rather than revenge, emphasizing forgiveness. Mandela's story exemplifies that true peace comes from within, cultivated through perseverance and strength in the face of adversity.

We all face difficult times, but it's how we respond that matters. Peace does not mean the absence of challenges, but the presence of inner strength to face them. Build your resilience so that you can maintain peace even in adversity. We often think that peace means a life free from challenges and difficulties. But that's a myth. Challenges are an inevitable part of life, and they can arise at any moment. The key is not to avoid them, but to develop the inner strength to face them head-on.

Inner fortitude is the foundation of peace. It's the ability to remain calm, focused, and resilient in the face of adversity. When we cultivate inner fortitude, we build our capacity to handle challenges with grace and ease. We develop a sense of inner strength that allows us to navigate difficult times with confidence and poise.

Practice self-awareness and introspection by developing a growth mindset and embrace challenges as opportunities for growth. Cultivate gratitude and focus on the present moment, build a support network of positive relationships and practice mindfulness and meditation to develop inner calm and clarity

Building inner fortitude is the key to maintaining peace in adversity. It's not about avoiding challenges, but about developing the inner strength to face them head-on. By cultivating inner fortitude, we can build resilience, navigate difficult times with ease, and maintain peace and calm in the midst of chaos.

Law 38

FIND JOY IN SERVICE

"The best way to find yourself is to lose yourself in the service of others." - Mahatma Gandhi

Mother Teresa, known for her selfless service, provides a powerful example of finding joy in helping others. In 1950, she founded the Missionaries of Charity in Calcutta, dedicating her life to the poorest of the poor. Mother Teresa's unwavering commitment to service exemplified her belief that joy arises from compassion.

She tended to the sick, fed the hungry, and provided shelter for the homeless, often finding joy in the simplest acts of kindness. Her life reminds us that true peace and fulfillment come from lifting others, demonstrating that in serving others, we also serve ourselves.

We're often told that the key to happiness lies in self-care and self-focus. And while taking care of ourselves is important, it's not enough. When we focus solely on our own needs and desires, we can become trapped in a cycle of selfishness and dissatisfaction. That is because true peace and fulfillment come not from getting what we want, but from giving to others. When we focus on the well-being of others, we transcend our own troubles and find a sense of purpose and peace.

Serving others has a profound impact on our lives. It shifts our focus away from our own problems and onto the needs of others. Gives us a sense of purpose and meaning, connects us with others and builds community. It increases feelings of empathy and compassion and brings a sense of joy and fulfillment. Service to others is a source of deep peace. By focusing on the well-being of others, you transcend your own troubles and find a sense

Finding joy in service is a powerful way to experience deep peace and fulfillment. By focusing on the well-being of others, we transcend our own troubles and find a sense of purpose and peace. Remember, true peace comes not from getting what we want, but from giving to others. So, start serving today and discover the joy and peace that comes from putting others first.

Law 39

AVOID UNNECESSARY CONFLICT

"The greatest glory in living lies not in never falling, but in rising every time we fall." - Nelson Mandela

During the tumultuous period of the American Revolution, the Founding Fathers faced numerous conflicts. Benjamin Franklin, known for his diplomatic skills, understood the importance of avoiding unnecessary conflict. When tensions escalated between loyalists and patriots, Franklin often advocated for dialogue rather than confrontation.

His ability to navigate conflicts with wisdom and restraint contributed to the eventual formation of a unified nation. Franklin's approach exemplifies that true strength lies not in fighting every battle but in discerning which conflicts are worth engaging in for the greater good.

Conflict can be exhausting emotionally, mentally, and physically. When we engage in unnecessary conflict, we waste time and energy on unproductive arguments, damage relationships and reputations, create stress and anxiety and miss out on opportunities for growth and connection. How do you know when to stand your ground and when to step back? Here are some practical tips;

- Ask yourself if the issue is worth fighting for

- Consider the potential consequences of conflict

- Look for alternative solutions and compromises

- Practice active listening and empathy

- Take time to reflect and calm down before reacting

Not all battles are worth fighting. Recognize when to stand your ground and when to step back. Peace often requires the wisdom to choose your conflicts wisely. Choosing your battles wisely is a key component of living a peaceful and fulfilling life. By avoiding unnecessary conflict and focusing on what truly matters, you can;

- Reduce stress and anxiety

- Build stronger relationships

- Increase our sense of calm and well-being

- Make a more positive impact on the world around us

Remember that peace often requires the wisdom to choose your conflicts wisely. So, take a step back, breathe, and ask yourself;

is this battle worth fighting.

Law 40

RELEASE THE NEED
FOR CONTROL

"The more you struggle to live, the less you live. Give up your struggle and float." - Alan Watts

During the Great Depression, President Franklin D. Roosevelt faced immense challenges. The economic crisis led to widespread uncertainty and fear. Rather than attempting to control the uncontrollable, Roosevelt chose to focus on the actions that could bring about positive change. His New Deal policies aimed to provide relief, recovery, and reform, acknowledging that some circumstances were beyond his control.

By fostering hope and encouraging collective action, Roosevelt demonstrated that releasing the need for control can lead to empowerment. His leadership during this trying time exemplifies that peace can be found in acceptance and proactive response rather than resistance.

Have you ever felt like you're constantly trying to hold onto control, only to find that it's slipping through your hands like sand. Most of us have tried to micromanage every aspect of our lives, only to end up feeling anxious, stressed, and utterly exhausted. Much of the anxiety that disrupts peace comes from the desire to control the uncontrollable. Release this need, and accept life as it unfolds. In surrender, peace is found.

We often think that if we can just control every aspect of our lives, we'll be safe, happy, and at peace. But the truth is, control is an illusion. Life is unpredictable, and no matter how hard we try, we can't control everything. So, why do we keep trying, you may ask? Often, it's because we're afraid of the unknown. We're afraid that if we let go of control, everything will fall apart. But the opposite is true. When we release the need for control, we open ourselves up to new possibilities, new experiences, and new growth.

Surrender is not about giving up; it's about letting go. It's about acknowledging that there are things beyond our control and trusting that everything will work out as it should. When we surrender, we;

- Reduce anxiety and stress
- Increase feelings of peace and calm
- Open ourselves up to new experiences and growth
- Build resilience and trust in the universe

You can start surrendering and releasing the need for control by practicing mindfulness and presence, letting go of the need for perfection, embracing uncertainty and the unknown. Trust in the universe and its plans and take small steps towards surrender every day.

Releasing the need for control is a journey, not a destination. It takes time, patience, and practice. But the payoff is worth it: peace, calm, and a deeper trust in the universe.

Law 41

FIND BALANCE IN ALL THINGS

"Balance is not something you find, it's something you create." - Jana Kingsford

Akira struggled with finding balance in her life. She would often oscillate between extremes, either working too much or playing too much, and found herself feeling drained and unfulfilled. One day, Akira was reminded of the importance of finding balance in all things.

Epictetus wrote, "Moderation is the best policy." Akira realized that her extremes were rooted in her own inner imbalance and lack of self-awareness. She began to practice self-reflection and moderation, finding a middle ground between work and play, rest and activity.

As Akira found balance in all things, she discovered a sense of harmony and contentment that she had never known before. She was no longer drained or unfulfilled, but felt energized and purposeful.

Are you tired of feeling like you're constantly teetering on the edge of chaos? Like you're juggling a million different balls in the air and just waiting for one to drop? You're not alone. We've all been there, trying to navigate the ups and downs of life while maintaining some semblance of peace and sanity.

Peace is the equilibrium between extremes. Strive for balance in your life, between work and rest, solitude and socializing, giving and receiving. Balance is the key to sustained peace.

We often find ourselves swinging between extremes; working too much and then crashing, socializing nonstop and then needing alone time, giving too much and then feeling drained. But these extremes can lead to burnout, exhaustion, and a sense of inner turmoil.

That's because extremes are, by definition, unbalanced. They're like a seesaw with one side weighed down and the other side flying high. And when we're living in extremes, we're constantly trying to find our footing, constantly trying to adjust to the latest shift. Balance, on the other hand, is like a perfectly balanced scale. Both sides are equal, and the result is peace, harmony, and stability. When we strive for balance in our lives, we reduce stress and anxiety. We experience increase feelings of calm and well-being, improve our relationships and communication, boost our productivity and creativity and enhance our overall sense of peace and happiness

You can find balance in your life by setting boundaries between work and rest. Prioritize self-care and alone time. Practice mindfulness and presence. Learn to say no and set healthy limits. And build meaningful relationships and connections Finding balance in all things is a journey, not a destination. It takes time, effort, and practice. But the payoff is worth it: sustained peace, harmony, and stability in a chaotic world. You don't have to be perfect. You don't have to have it all together. In fact, trying to do so will only lead to more stress and anxiety. Take a deep breath, let go of the need for extremes, and strive for balance in all things. Your peace and well-being depend on it.

Law 42

EMBRACE THE PRESENT WITH GRATITUDE

"The present moment is the only moment available to us, and it is the door to all moments." - Thich Nhat Hanh

Kaito struggled with living in the present. He would often find himself lost in thoughts of the past or worries about the future, and felt disconnected from the world around him. One day, while reading the teachings of Epictetus, Kaito was reminded of the importance of embracing the present with gratitude.

Epictetus wrote, "Make the best use of the present." Kaito realized that his mind was always wandering, and he was missing out on the beauty and wonder of the present moment. He began to practice mindfulness and gratitude, focusing on the sights, sounds, and sensations of the present.

As Kaito embraced the present with gratitude, he found a sense of peace and connection that he had never known before. He was no longer lost in thoughts of the past or worries about the future, but felt fully alive and engaged in gratitude. Kaito had learned to make the best use of the present, and it had brought him greater peace and happiness.

A way to unlock peace and find gratitude in the present moment is a simple yet profound concept; embracing the present with gratitude. We often find ourselves stuck in the past, reliving memories and regrets. Or we get caught up in worries about the future, anxious about what might happen. But this cycle of regret and worry is a trap, it keeps us from experiencing peace in the present moment.

Regret and worry are like two heavy weights that hold us back, preventing us from moving forward. They keep us stuck in a cycle of negativity, unable to find gratitude for what we have. Gratitude is the antidote to regret and worry. When we focus on what we're grateful for, we begin to shift our perspective. We start to see the good in our lives, the beauty in the present moment.

When you embrace the present with gratitude, you reduce your stress and anxiety. You will see an increased feeling of peace and calm, improved relationships and connections, enhanced overall sense of well-being and joy and contentment in the present moment

The present moment is where peace resides. Embrace it fully, with gratitude for what it offers. By grounding yourself in the present, you diminish the regrets of the past and the worries of the future.

To embrace the present with gratitude;

- Practice mindfulness and presence

- Keep a gratitude journal

- Share gratitude with others

- Focus on the small joys in life

- Cultivate a sense of wonder and awe

Embracing the present with gratitude is a journey, not a destination. It takes time, effort, and practice. But the payoff is worth it: peace, calm, and a deeper appreciation for life. You don't have to be held back by regret and worry. You can break free and find peace in the present moment. So, take a deep breath, let go of the past and future, and embrace the present with gratitude. Your peace and well-being depend on it.

Law 43

LISTEN MORE THAN YOU SPEAK

"Nature has given us two ears, two eyes, and but one tongue-to the end that we should hear and see more than we speak." - Socrates

Mitchel struggled with listening. She would often find herself interrupting others, or thinking about her own response while others were speaking, and felt like she was missing out on deep connections and insights. She was hearing but never listening. One day, she and one of her friends were having a discussion, she was hearing but was not listening. She wanted to share her own views.

Two days later, she received a phone call from her friend, who was calling to ask if she went to the interview. Mitchel was confused, "which interview?" she asked. Apparently, her friend mentioned that she recommended her for a job and she was to go for an interview. She missed the opportunity because she was not a good listener.

Mitchel realized that her tendency to speak over others was

rooted in her own ego and desire to be heard and it has tendencies to steal her opportunities. She began to practice active listening, focusing on fully understanding others before responding.

As Mitchel listened more than she spoke, she found a sense of peace and understanding that she had never known before. She was no longer missing out on deep connections and insights, and felt like she was truly hearing.

Listening is something that is often overlooked but incredibly powerful. In a world where everyone wants to be heard, it's easy to forget that listening is just as important as speaking. But trust me, it's a game-changer.

Peace is often found in listening. By truly hearing others, you foster understanding and connection, reducing the likelihood of conflict.

Listening helps us avoid misunderstandings and miscommunications. How many times have you gotten into an argument or conflict because someone misinterpreted what you said? Yeah, it's frustrating. But when we take the time to truly listen to each other, we can clear up those misunderstandings and get on the same page.

Listening also helps us build deeper connections with others. When someone feels heard and understood, they are more likely to open up and share their thoughts and feelings with us. And that is where the magic happens, that is where we build trust, empathy, and strong relationships.

You may be saying, "But I'm a good listener! I hear what people are saying." And that's great! However, there's a difference between hearing and truly listening. Hearing is passive; listening is active. When we actively listen, we're engaged, focused, and present. We're not just waiting for our turn to speak; we're fully absorbed in what the other person is saying.

Law 44

A L I G N Y O U R L I F E
W I T H Y O U R
P R I N C I P L E S

"Integrity is doing the right thing even when no one is watching." - C.S. Lewis

J ude was the team lead in my department. We worked in marketing and advertising. We were a closely knitted department, this is because we spent a lot of time working together and our retreats were always a highlight. My team had 10 members and news goes around pretty fast.

After Jude was made Head of department, he called a meeting to lay down rules that every member must abide with. We all agreed to cooperate and support each other. However, Jude flaunted all those rules he laid down by the end of the month and kept reprimanding other members of the department who flaunted the rules.

One day, one of the interns came late, he arrived the same time Jude arrived. We all knew he had an emergency and that Jude was going to reprimand him despite the fact that he was not upholding his own principle. We decided to confront him and ask why he was not following the rules that we should.

He was not happy with us but apologized. He later called a meeting where he apologized again and promised to live by his own principles. He began to practice integrity, aligning his actions with his values and principles.

As Jude aligned his life with his principles, he found a sense of peace and integrity that he had never known before. He was no longer torn between his values and his desires, but felt like he was living a life of purpose and meaning.

Are you tired of feeling like you are living a life that isn't truly yours? Do you often find yourself compromising your values and beliefs to fit in or achieve success? You are not alone. Many of us struggle to align our lives with our principles, leading to feelings of disconnection, guilt, and inner turmoil.

Peace comes from living in harmony with your beliefs. Let your principles guide your actions consistently, and you will find inner peace and external harmony. When we live a life that's misaligned with our principles, we can experience inner conflict and guilt, disconnection from our true selves, external conflict and harmony with others and a sense of purposelessness and meaninglessness

On the other hand, when we align our lives with our principles, we can experience inner peace and calm, a sense of purpose and direction, external harmony and stronger relationships and increased self-trust and confidence

You can align your life with your principles by;

- Identify your core values and beliefs

- Assess your current life and identify areas of misalignment

- Set boundaries and prioritize self-care

- Make intentional decisions that align with your principles

- Practice mindfulness and self-reflection

Living a life of alignment is a journey. It takes time, effort, and commitment, but the payoff is worth it: inner peace, external harmony, and a life that truly reflects your values and principles. You have the power to create a life that aligns with your principles. Don't settle for anything less.

Law 45

MAINTAIN A GRATEFUL PERSPECTIVE

"Gratitude unlocks the fullness of life. It turns what we have into enough, and more." - Melody Beattie.

A young poet named Chloe struggled with maintaining a grateful perspective. She would often find herself focusing on what was lacking in her life, and felt like she was never truly happy. One day, while reading the teachings of Epictetus, Chloe was reminded of the importance of gratitude.

Epictetus wrote, "He is a wise man who does not grieve for the things which he has not, but rejoices for those which he has." Chloe realized that her focus on lack was rooted in her own negativity and dissatisfaction. She began to practice gratitude, focusing on the good things in her life and expressing thanks for what she had.

As Chloe maintained a grateful perspective, she found a sense of peace and contentment that she had never known before. She was no longer focused on what was lacking, but felt like she had enough and was truly happy. Chloe had learned to focus on the good, and it had brought her greater peace and happiness.

We are often caught up in a mindset of scarcity and dissatisfaction at one time or the other. But what if I told you that there is a simple yet profound way to shift your focus and find peace and abundance? It starts with gratitude. Gratitude shifts your focus from lack to abundance. Regularly reflect on what you are grateful for, and you will find that peace follows naturally from a heart full of thanks. When we focus on what's lacking in our lives, we can experience dissatisfaction, discontentment, anxiety, stress, comparison, envy, a sense of scarcity and limitation

When we focus on what we are grateful for, we can experience peace, contentment, joy, happiness, abundance, prosperity and sense of trust and faith

You can build and nurture a grateful perspective by following the steps below.

- Keep a gratitude journal

- Share gratitude with others

- Reflect on your blessings daily

- Practice mindfulness and presence

- Celebrate the small wins

Gratitude is a powerful tool for shifting our focus from lack to abundance. By regularly reflecting on what we are thankful for, we can find peace, joy, and contentment. Gratitude is a muscle that needs to be exercised regularly to see results. Start today and watch your life transform in amazing ways.

Law 46

TRUST THE PROCESS OF LIFE.

"The universe has a way of revealing itself to those who are willing to listen and trust in its unfolding."
- Unknown

Alone, I sat in my small apartment, surrounded by papers and pens, trying to plan every detail of my life. I had a five-year plan, a ten-year plan, and even a twenty-year plan. I was determined to control every aspect of my life, to ensure that everything went exactly as I wanted. But life had other plans.

As I sat there, poring over my plans, I received an unexpected phone call. It was my boss, telling me that the company was downsizing and my job was being eliminated. I was devastated. All my plans, all my control, seemed to be slipping away.

I spent the next few days in a daze, feeling lost and uncertain about my future. But then I stumbled upon a quote that changed everything: "It's not what happens to you, but how you react to it that matters." - Epictetus

I realized that I had been so focused on controlling every aspect of my life that I had forgotten to trust in the process. I had forgotten to trust that life was unfolding according to its own rhythm, and that every experience, every setback, and every success was leading me closer to my highest good.

I took a deep breath and let go of my need for control. I started to trust in the universe's plan, to trust that everything was working in my favor. And slowly but surely, I began to feel a sense of peace and calm that I had never felt before.

I started to see that life was not about controlling every detail, but about trusting in the flow. I started to see that every experience, every setback, and every success was an opportunity for growth and learning. Life unfolds according to its own rhythm. Trust in this process, even when it diverges from your plans. Peace comes from accepting life's flow rather than resisting it.

When we trust in the process of life, we

- Reduce stress and anxiety

- Increase feelings of peace and calm

- Improve our ability to adapt to change

- Enhance our resilience and ability to bounce back

- Align ourselves with the natural flow of life

Trusting the process is not easy and takes discipline. You have to be deliberate and practice mindfulness and presence, let go of your need for control and trust in the universe's plan. You should also focus on the present moment and build a sense of curiosity and wonder. Trusting the process of life is a journey, not a destination. It takes time, effort, and practice. But the payoff is worth it: peace, calm, and a sense of alignment with the natural flow of life. Remember, it's not what happens to you, but how you react to it that matters.

Law 47

AVOID THE PITFALL OF PERFECTIONISM

"Perfection is the enemy of good." - Voltaire

A young artist named Theo struggled with perfectionism. He would often find himself spending hours on a single detail, trying to make it flawless, and felt like he was never truly satisfied with his work. One day, frustrated and exhausted, he stepped back to take a breath. His eyes fell upon a painting he had abandoned months ago– a vibrant explosion of colors, wild and free, yet imperfect. It whispered to him, reminding him of the joy he once felt while creating.

With a deep breath, Theo picked up his brush and began to paint again, not with the goal of perfection, but with the intention of expression. Each stroke was liberating, every color a path to his journey toward embracing his imperfections.

As the sun dipped below the horizon, Theo stepped back to admire his work. It wasn't perfect but it was real, a reflection of his heart. In that moment, he realized that true beauty lies not in flawlessness, but in the courage to embrace his imperfections.

Epictetus wrote, "It's not about being the best, it's about being better than you were yesterday." He realized that while he wasn't his best yet, he has become better than when he first started. With that, he smiled and got ready to paint his next story.

Perfection is, by nature, an illusion. What one person considers perfect may not resonate with another. When we set an unrealistically high standard for ourselves, we inevitably set ourselves up for failure. Each time we fall short, we experience feelings of inadequacy, frustration and disappointment.

Perfectionism often breeds comparison. We look at others and see their successes, their polished lives, and we feel inadequate. But remember, everyone is fighting their own battles behind the scenes. Instead of comparing ourselves to others, let's celebrate our unique journeys. Focus on your progress, not someone else's perfection.

Embracing imperfection can be liberating. It allows us to be authentic, to take risks, and to learn from our experiences. When we let go of the need to be perfect, we open ourselves up to new possibilities and deeper connections with others.

Law 48

CULTIVATE AN ATTITUDE OF ACCEPTANCE

"Strength does not come from physical capacity. It comes from an indomitable will." - Mahatma Gandhi

Mia woke up to the soft light filtering through her bedroom window. It was a Saturday, and she had planned a day filled with errands. As she stretched and took a deep breath, she reminded herself of her intention for the day; to embrace acceptance in all situations, no matter how challenging they might be.

After a quick breakfast, Mia hopped into her car, ready to tackle her to-do list. The first stop was the grocery store. As she navigated through the aisles, she noticed a long line at the checkout. Instead of feeling frustrated, she took a moment to observe her surroundings. She noticed a young mother struggling to calm her baby and an elderly man searching for change in his pocket.

Instead of letting impatience take over, Mia smiled at the mother and offered a few words of encouragement. "You are doing great!" The mother smiled back, visibly relieved. This small act of kindness reminded Mia that everyone faces their own challenges and sometimes, a little acceptance can go a long way.

After shopping, Mia went back home to continue her chores for the day. As the sun began to set, she reflected on her day and how acceptance transformed her experience at the grocery store. She realized that accepting the unexpected in a calm manner has allowed her to connect more deeply with others and herself.

Acceptance is the foundation of peace. Accept yourself, others, and the world as they are, without the need to change or control. In acceptance, you find the deepest and most enduring peace.

Acceptance is not about being passive or resigned; it is about embracing reality with open arms. When we accept what is; we free ourselves from the burden of resistance and unwanted worry and create space for growth and healing.

By accepting others for who they are, we release the need to control or change them, allowing us to build deeper, more meaningful connections. And by accepting yourself, you quiet the inner voices and awaken to your true potential.

As you journey towards cultivating acceptance, remember;

- It's okay to not be okay.

- Life is unpredictable but that is what makes it beautiful!

- You are enough, exactly as you are.

- Do you at all times. Don't be tempted to change to fit into someone's idea of a perfect person.

Remember, acceptance is a journey, not a destination. Embrace the present moment, with all its imperfections and uncertainties. By cultivating an attitude of acceptance, your life blooms from a gray colored aura of self-hate to a vibrant tapestry of peace, compassion and understanding. You also gain the power to uplift those around you. So, take that first step today, and discover the peace that awaits.

About the Author

Victor O. Carl is the pen name of a visionary researcher and author whose mission is to empower individuals to unlock their full potential. With a background rooted in extensive research and a passion for personal growth, Carl has authored several transformative books.

His first book, *The 48 Laws of Mental Power*, takes readers deep into the unseen forces driving human behavior, unlocking strategies to sharpen the mind and fortify inner resilience. Carl continued his quest for self-mastery in *The 48 Laws of Habit Mastery*, delivering timeless methods to transform routines and habits into tools of success. With *The 48 Laws of Money*, Carl demystifies the secrets of wealth-building, bridging psychology and financial wisdom, while *The 48 Laws of Peace* offers readers a path to inner tranquility in an increasingly chaotic world.

Carl's books are not just guides but manuals for survival in a world designed to overwhelm the individual. Drawing from his profound experiences and deep research, he challenges readers to transcend the limitations imposed by society and their own conditioning. His work is crafted for those who are ready to break free, master themselves, and achieve lasting transformation. You can Visit his website below to know more.

www.48lol.com

Acknowledgments

I am deeply grateful to my family, especially my wife and kids (Videl, Vishal, and Valen), and to my friends for their unwavering support and belief in my vision. To the mentors and thinkers whose ideas shaped these works—thank you for your invaluable guidance.

A heartfelt thanks to my readers, whose curiosity and dedication to personal growth inspire me to continue writing. These books are for all who seek mastery over their minds, habits, and lives.

Thank you for being part of this journey.